School Library
Makerspaces in Action

SCHOOL LIBRARY MAKERSPACES IN ACTION

Heather Moorefield-Lang, Editor

LIBRARIES
UNLIMITED™
An Imprint of ABC-CLIO, LLC
Santa Barbara, California • Denver, Colorado

Library of Congress Cataloging-in-Publication Data

Names: Moorefield-Lang, Heather, editor.
Title: School library makerspaces in action / Heather Moorefield-Lang, editor.
Description: Santa Barbara, California : Libraries Unlimited, An Imprint of ABC-CLIO, LLC [2018] | Includes bibliographical references and index.
Identifiers: LCCN 2017043186 (print) | LCCN 2017060507 (ebook) | ISBN 9781440856976 (ebook) | ISBN 9781440856969 (pbk)
Subjects: LCSH: Makerspaces in libraries. | School libraries—Activity programs. | Instructional materials centers—Activity programs.
Classification: LCC Z716.37 (ebook) | LCC Z716.37.S36 2018 (print) | DDC 025.5—dc23
LC record available at https://lccn.loc.gov/2017043186

ISBN: 978-1-4408-5696-9 (paperback)
      978-1-4408-5697-6 (ebook)

22 21 20 19 18   1 2 3 4 5

This book is also available as an eBook.

Libraries Unlimited
An Imprint of ABC-CLIO, LLC

ABC-CLIO, LLC
130 Cremona Drive, P.O. Box 1911
Santa Barbara, California 93116-1911
www.abc-clio.com

This book is printed on acid-free paper ∞
Manufactured in the United States of America

Contents

Foreword

In Chicago after the great fire of 1871, amid new technologies like the electric elevator and plummeting steel prices, a set of architects rethought the city skyline. They had no kits, no prefab instructions. Instead they mixed design influences, new construction tools, and a resurgent local interest in Chicago to build skyscrapers. What they intended as a bold melding of pragmatism and idealistic vision ended up changing society. The skyscraper, along with the advent of reliable phone systems, allowed corporations to grow larger and to coordinate global enterprises under a single, albeit lofty roof. This created a new urbanism that shifted populations from the countryside to the city.

What is remarkable about this process is that it began with a change in thinking. Old norms of how things had to be done were thrown out. New relationships of like-minded artisans and engineers came together and realized they could create, not simply implement.

The analogy may seem to be clear to the world of making and maker spaces. However, that is a secondary application. The primary one is that it took a corps of dedicated facilitators who helped weave a new view and new thinking. In Chicago there were students, demonstrations, tours, workshops. In our schools, with classroom teachers increasingly scheduled and curriculum shaped by high-stakes testing, school librarians have an opportunity to create spaces of experimentation, design, and new thinking.

This is not a new mission for school librarians. They have always nurtured makers—makers of new ideas and new narratives. They have always sought to supplement curriculum with inquiry—to amplify imagination and instill a sense of power that fuses math, science, history, and language into new realities. They have done this without a kit, a blueprint, or a predefined path but always with purpose.

This book, then, is more about you, the school librarian, than the spaces you build or the students you inspire. You are the makers.

Dr. David Lankes
Director, School of Library and Information Science
University of South Carolina, Columbia

Introduction

WHAT IS THIS BOOK ABOUT?

In one word, this book is about makerspaces, but, truly, that is too simple; a robust selection of books are already available on that topic. Overall, this book is about makerspaces in school libraries and in school library partnerships. To delve deeper, this book is based on case studies of maker learning spaces in school libraries (and a few public libraries), looking at maker librarians and how they are effectively implementing maker activities, creativity, and collaboration in their library spaces. Libraries have always been a location for the creation of knowledge. They have always been a place to build, create, and collaborate. Adding in the idea or a space for making is a natural one for libraries and librarians (Willingham and de Boer, 2015).

The content of this book is organized into four parts: Early Grades, Middle Grades, Upper Grades, concluding with Collaborations, Training, and More. I describe each chapter as a case study because you as the reader are getting a glimpse into the educational practice of a particular person or group.

#MakerMonday: Inspiring Students to Think with Their Hands, by Stacy Brown, takes us through the process of creating a makingspace using hi-tech and low-tech resources. Stacy Hammer's chapter, *Wide Open Spaces: Creating a School Makerspace in an Open School*, discusses the maker movement in libraries particularly at the elementary or lower grade levels. IdaMae Craddock, in her chapter *Makers Gonna Make*, discusses a library's journey from traditional maker, while Jennifer Tazerouti takes us through her own journey of maker discovery in her chapter, *A Makerspace Journey of the Middle and Elementary Kind*. Sarah Justice talks about how technology implementation in her school led to the creation of a makerspace in her library in *The Makerspace Evolution*. Phil Goerner and Lucas Maxwell both discuss student-driven

makerspaces in their chapters *Student-Led Makerspaces* and *Stepping Back: Letting Students Lead the Makerspace*. Gina Seymour takes us on a journey of inclusiveness in her chapter *The Inclusive Makerspace: Working with English Language Learners and Special Education Students*. The book wraps up with chapters on training and collaborations. Laura Fleming shares ideas for maker training in her chapter *Maker Professional Learning for Educators*. Jeroen de Boer, Roxanne Spray, and Melissa Crenshaw write about their public library and school library partnerships in Impact through Connection at School*: Public Libraries Creating Impact by Bringing Digital Literacies and Maker Skills into the Classroom* as well as *Shared Spaces and Makerspaces: A Public Library and School Library Partnership*.

Every chapter in *School Library Makerspaces in Action* offers real-life case studies in how making happens in libraries and educational settings from the experiences of the authors. Useful ideas abound, and it is hoped that readers will walk away with a wide range of ideas for their learning location.

MAKERSPACES AND SCHOOL LIBRARIES

Making as a culture has grown in popularity particularly in libraries over the past five years. Spaces to make, or "makerspaces," are locations to create, build, craft, collaborate, and explore. Children, adults, and families have been very excited to take part in the maker learning locations offered at libraries, museums, and other environments of instruction over the past few years (Halverson and Sheridan, 2014). Laura Fleming defines a makerspace as, "A metaphor for a unique learning environment that encourages tinkering, play, and open-ended exploration for all" (Fleming, 2016, para. 2). These are locations, sometimes fixed, sometimes mobile, that have the ability to add a wonderful learning experience in a library and other educational settings.

When we look at Bloom's Taxonomy, we in a library are already working at the levels of remembering and understanding various topics and information. We as librarians are also adept at instruction in analyzing and evaluating information, especially when we are working with our students on their information literacy skills. What about the top of the Bloom's Pyramid? What about creation (Bieraugel and Neill, 2017)? In libraries we can reach that goal with projects and peer educator collaboration, but think of what can be achieved with making, creation, and maker learning spaces. Think about the group work, the research projects, and integration that can occur, as well as the critical thinking that can be achieved. Surely something to ponder as you make your way through this book.

AUDIENCE

I envision the readers of this book to be school librarians, classroom teachers, preservice librarians, professors of library science, as well as librarians in other fields such as academic and public. In actuality, this book is for anyone looking to find ideas and concepts in the area of making, makerspaces, hackerspaces, fab labs, and DIY locations and how they might be used in libraries and education. We have authors from around the world represented in this book, and we hope to address the needs of international readers as well. Every chapter written for this book had a specific audience in mind because the authors worked with a certain population. We know though that, with only a little fine-tuning and imagination, many of these ideas could be used throughout all levels, disciplines, and subjects in K–12 education and could carry over into higher education as well. This book was written for the express purpose of generating and sharing ideas, as well as to optimistically inspire our readers to think about maker learning locations and their potential uses in libraries and classrooms.

REFERENCES

Bieraugel, Mark, and Stern Neill. "Ascending Bloom's Pyramid: Fostering Student Creativity and Innovation in Academic Library Spaces." *College & Research Libraries 78*, no. 1 (2017): 35–52.

Fleming, Laura. "Themed Making." *Worlds of Learning.* Blog. May 14, 2016. http://worlds-of-learning.com/2016/05/13/themed-making/

Halverson, Erica Rosenfeld, and Kimberly Sheridan. "The Maker Movement in Education." *Harvard Educational Review 84*, no. 4 (2014): 495–504.

Willingham, Theresa, and Jeroen de Boer. *Makerspaces in Libraries.* Vol. 4. Lanham, MD: Rowman & Littlefield, 2015.

Part I

Early Grades

1

#MakerMonday: Inspiring Students to Think with Their Hands

Stacy Brown

INTRODUCTION

Maker Monday all started with a hashtag. As an independent Jewish day school with approximately 600 students on two campuses, The Davis Academy is always seeking innovative ways to bring our community into the classroom to gain support, to encourage understanding, and to make connections. This is one reason why each of our grade levels has a unique grade-level Twitter hashtag and 100% of our faculty has a Twitter handle. With this in mind, the idea of #MakerMonday was born. An investment in Lego® robotics really brought to life the concept of thinking with your hands at our school.

As part of a technology and science funding initiative, we purchased several tubs of Legos for education, including the simple machine set and the community helper set, both of which tied in nicely to our curriculum in kindergarten prep and second grade. After purchasing these, we also purchased the Lego Robotics WeDo kits and the Lego Robotics Mindstorm kits. The Lego Robotics WeDo kits are geared for ages 7 and up and introduce students to building robots that incorporate sensors and motors. Using the drag-and-drop Lego WeDo software, students can begin to understand how to program the robots to move and make noise. According to the MIT Media Lab blog, the Lego Robotics Mindstorm kits grew out of 20 years of research collaboration between The

3

Lego Group and Massachusetts Institute of Technology. The kits are designed for ages 10 and up and include a programmable brick, more complex build options, and a larger variety of motors and sensors than WeDo kits. The Lego Mindstorm programming language is more challenging than the Lego WeDo version. The media team was motivated to see that these resources were put to good use. According to Tony Wagner, author of *Creating Innovators: The Making of Young People Who Will Change the World* (2012), "Research shows that human beings are born with an innate desire to explore, experiment, and imagine new possibilities—in a word, to innovate" (p. 26). While structured learning in classrooms is important for many students, so is unstructured time to tinker, problem-solve, and challenge one's own understanding of the environment. As Kristen Swanson, cofounder of EdCamp, has stated, "[A] well-designed learning experience for adults requires space and time." She notes that this is why so many educators rediscover their hobbies over the winter break. She designates this as the "white space," or creating the conditions in which learning can take place (Swanson, personal communication, January 24, 2015). The mission behind Maker Monday was driven by this notion of creating the white space for students. Maker Monday would become the white space, or the time and the space in which students could explore and create using Legos, including Lego Robotics. Word spread quickly about Maker Monday and in no time at all, it gained significant popularity in our school community.

IN THE BEGINNING

The Logistics

In developing Maker Monday, there were several challenges to consider. Timing, supervision, and buy-in were the first conditions that required exploration. In regard to the timing of Maker Monday, we would not gain buy-in from the teachers or from the parents if we asked to host Maker Monday during core instruction time. Hosting Maker Monday before an already early school day would penalize some students who simply could not arrive at school earlier than the 7:55 start time. We were able to solve timing and buy-in by hosting our first Maker Monday during recess, as an experiment. Attending Maker Monday during recess was optional, but the event had a large turnout on that first day. It also made for a quieter recess duty for the teachers on the playground. Maker Monday is particularly popular on a rainy day. In addition to gaining buy-in from the homeroom teachers so as not to disrupt their core learning time or impose upon their schedules, we were able to gain buy-in from the parents through not only the students' enthusiasm when they got into their cars to go home at the end of the day but also through the grade-level Twitter hashtags. I made a point of tweeting #MakerMonday with each grade-level hashtag, such as #DavisK, along with images and brief explanations of our projects. This gave parents a "window" into the creative opportunities for their students. While recess is a highly coveted part of the day, Maker Monday brought new meaning to playtime.

Supervision was a crucial consideration as well. Once Maker Monday quickly gained momentum, I was given permission to bring in our part-time information technology (IT) coordinator as an extra set of hands. Although the media special-ists and the IT professionals report to different individu-als in separate departments, this was a positive way to bring the two departments together. Additionally, the IT

IT Coordinator Assisting with #MakerMonday.

coordinator had been able to create a separate electronics and hardware sta-tion in which students can choose to dissect old computers, e-readers, cam-eras, and phones. An unexpected outcome for the IT coordinator was that this proved to be a nice change of pace in the middle of his day.

Our media center is the heart of our school. It is anything but quiet, it is hopping with action, and it is situated in the middle of our school. I needed to find an alternative location for Maker Monday while emphasizing that this pro-gramming was an extension of our media center. At one end of our building was an empty classroom that had been slated to become an Idea Lab. It was getting a makeover with boldly colored seating pods, a new rug, and idea paint on the walls. As with anything, when schools invest in new spaces, their usage is imperative to gain support for additional spaces and resources in the future. The Idea Lab was determined to be the perfect home for Maker Monday. Having the idea paint on the walls has been amazing for planning designs, sharing positive quotes, providing instructions, and dividing up the placement of maker stations.

The Hook

Tapping into your own personal inspiration is key to successful projects. In our case, we have 25 minutes of Maker Monday time with the students. The question became, "How can we create meaningful learning opportunities ripe with exploration in only 25 minutes?" First, I had to consider what excited me because my enthusiasm was sure to translate into the execution of the proj-ects. At the same time, I needed to appeal to a variety of makers. After hooking the students with Lego Robotics, I made sure to integrate crafts as an additional station. A crafty corner of pipe cleaners, feathers, pompoms, markers, and con-struction paper was all that was needed to get the makers making. We had a group of students who created their own jewelry line with these crafts.

In order to differentiate the maker experience and help with crowd control, I also added the tinkering station, consisting of broken, donated electronics.

Students interested in hardware could dissect and explore the guts of computers, broken Kindles, and older digital cameras. The IT coordinator facilitated the tinkering giving the students a chance to interact with a different role model within the school. Having received ten first-generation programmable, app-enabled robotic balls, known as Spheros, from a parent who received them as a promotional item at work, we were also able to create a programming station in which students were challenged to program the Spheros to complete specific tasks using the Sphero's drag-and-drop programming app. Initially known as MacroLab, the app for Sphero is now known as SPRK Lightning Lab. The concept, however, is the same in that students use their drag-and-drop programming skills to control the behaviors of the Sphero. As a final option, a mini-maker challenge corner was offered. Some examples of mini-maker challenges included designing a house for a gnome, building a maze, and constructing a paper airplane, each with a slew of specific resources. Ultimately, the Maker Monday menu consisted of the following stations: tinkering, robotics, crafting, mini-maker challenges, and programming. Having a variety of stations helped not only to generate more interest but also with crowd control, so that students were spread throughout different areas of our Idea Lab.

We continued with this structure for the next several months, incorporating slight variations. For example, we added a Create a Chariot for your Sphero component to the Sphero programming station. I also had alternative plans for rainy days, at which time we could expect almost an entire grade level to attend Maker Monday. I became savvy with my supply orders so as to minimize the cost yet order supplies that had a big impact. I ordered 30 inexpensive 3D glasses on Amazon.com and had students create 3D books that they could take turns reading to one another with the use of the glasses. Using a red Sharpie, students wrote a story and illustrated their images. Then, using a blue Sharpie®, they outlined what they wrote and drew in red. The result was a 3D effect that could be appreciated with the use of the 3D glasses. Additionally, I ensured I had the tinkering station open and facilitated by the IT coordinator. This way, when students had questions or needed help, we had fewer stations to manage.

Creating 3D Books with Sharpies.

Maker Monday Becomes Mission Irresistible

Maker Monday marketed itself. The buzz from the students, the regular tweets, and the teacher appreciation translated into significant support. The admissions director ensured that the Idea Lab was a critical destination on a school tour. The administration made a point of ensuring visitors to our school got a glimpse of the action happening in the Idea Lab, and resources became easier to obtain. After the Lego Robotics, our next big purchase was littleBits®, which are magnetic blocks that can be snapped together to create circuits that include inputs and outputs to power unique inventions. Having seen littleBits at education conferences shortly after they came out, I was intrigued. We started with a basic littleBits kit and ultimately migrated to having two littleBits workshop sets, each of which can accommodate up to eight pairs of students working together. While I love the creativity that happens when you are limited in your resources and are therefore forced to be imaginative, littleBits proved to be a turning point in our school maker culture. The littleBits are accessible to all ages and therefore are the ultimate tool to differentiating maker education. The projects that my students have created with littleBits is a book unto itself. However, you can find many of the projects at The Davis Academy's 4th Grade Technology blog (2013).

After tweeting to littleBits all of the imaginative creations over the last couple of years, littleBits asked if we would be interested in becoming a chapter school. Being a chapter school has allowed us the opportunity to purchase more bits at a discount and to share our unique inventions and lessons on the littleBits Web site and has made us instantly aware of their monthly invention challenges. Each month, a group of our students will take the littleBits challenge, which has included creating a birthday-themed invention, a Harry Potter–style invention, and an invention that glows. We have won one challenge so far, and as a result, we were sent the littleBits Rule Your Room Kit as a reward.

After such success with littleBits, we purchased three Hummingbird Robotics Kits. Hummingbird robotics kits contain a controller, LED lights, motors, sensors, a power supply, a USB cable, and a screwdriver. Using cardboard and other craft supplies, students can design and build interactive robots that can move, talk, and light up. This was another game changer for us. When students realized that they could create anything and program it to move and light up, they were dazzled. The Hummingbird Robotics Kits make programming accessible for fourth graders and up. With a five-minute lesson on the microcomputer, the servos, sensors, and LED lights, and with emphasis on the importance of a good design, students can create impressive inventions out of cardboard. Having students work in pairs ensures that both students are engaged while being a part of the design/build process as well as the programming. We encourage diverse teams too since they bring different experiences to the planning process.

Once again, we made a point of tweeting our Hummingbird creations to the BirdBrain Technologies company at every opportunity. In time, we were chosen to pilot the Finch Robots, which were in beta. We took this very seriously! It provided an opportunity for our students to have a crucial role in a project much bigger than themselves. Starting at level one, students mastered the Snap programming language and ultimately improved their programming skills with the Finch. We created short videos for BirdBrain Technologies sharing our feedback on the Finch, empowering the students beyond the maker experience.

As our Maker Monday popularity and therefore our resources continued to grow, we were able to leverage the students' confidence in the value of attending Maker Monday. We had reached a point at which we could successfully create a combined low-tech/high-tech maker experience. In the beginning, it was a bigger decision for students to decide between recess on the playground versus Maker Monday in the Idea Lab. While we purposefully ensured a choice of high-tech or low-tech maker projects, we ultimately were able to blend the two to appeal to a wider audience in one project.

The Projects: Low Tech, High Tech, and Everything in Between

As with all creative processes, some weeks the ideas would flow whereas other weeks, it was more challenging to come up with meaningful projects that could be accomplished in 25-minute blocks. Enthusiasm on the part of the makerspace facilitator is key to enthusiasm on the part of the students. Students can sense the facilitator's level of passion for a particular project, which translates into the rollout of the project itself. The success of a project is obvious in the faces of the students and in their feedback during and after their visit to the makerspace. While we have not yet had a project that was not successful or fulfilling on some level, here are some of our most rewarding projects.

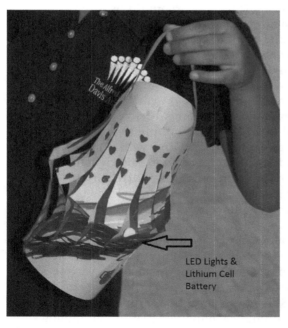

Chinese Lanterns

To date, this has been one of our most popular projects. The inspiration for this project came from a local event in which our community comes together with handmade lanterns and participates in a lantern parade throughout a historic part of Atlanta. Tapping into the unique events in one's own community can prove to inspire meaningful maker moments. Students drew patterns and designs on brightly colored paper, folded the paper in half, cut lines in the paper from the inside, and taped the paper together in a cylinder-like shape. Then, attaching a pipe cleaner handle on the top and

Chinese Lanterns with LED Lights and Lithium Batteries.

lithium batteries and LED lights on the inside, students were able to make their lanterns glow. Students who grasped the creation of these circuits quickly learned how to make switches for their lamps so that they could be turned on and off. Interestingly, students made time to attend the end of their recess so that they could form their own outdoor lantern parade.

Silent Movies

Integrating the tactile experience and the virtual experience, as previously mentioned, appeals to a variety of makers. The Silent Film Studio app created by Cateater, LLC, which sells for $0.99 for up to 19 apps or for $0.49 for 20 or more apps, allowed makers to merge the tactile and the virtual experience. Working in small groups of up to five, students created a storyboard using a storyboard template that was printed out for them on plain white paper. As an added benefit of generating some homegrown marketing for the media center and to cut back on the planning time, students in kindergarten prep through third grade were asked to create silent films about why they loved the media center. Upper elementary students were given the freedom to choose their topic.

Upon approval of their storyline, students were able to begin filming their movie in the Silent Film Studio app. Although I never know how many students may show up on any given day, I was able to break all of the students into groups of up to six with no more than eight students per group at a time. Having spent 7 minutes on their storyboard and 10 minutes filming, we were left with 8 minutes to share our videos, which was plenty of time. When the videos are processed within the app, they are created in fast motion so each video only takes about 30 seconds to view. The audience of moviemakers was enthralled watching each group's production. This is a low-prep, big-impact project that appeals to all types of makers.

Design Challenges

Serving up a menu of design challenges is a way to build in choice while making the maker experience manageable for the facilitator. Look around and take note of what supplies currently exist and can be relegated to a maker activity. Examples of design challenges at The Davis Academy include creating a night light with

Creating a Silent Film with the Silent Film Studio App.

littleBits, creating a comic strip about a science project gone wrong, building a simple machine out of Legos, making a favorite animal in origami, building a three-dimensional structure out of sticky notes and creating a story to accompany the structure, and designing and drawing a unique robot on the wall using idea paint and creating a name and a backstory for the robot. Students appreciate when choice is built into their maker experience.

Beyond Hour of Code

As more and more schools are integrating coding into their curriculum, seeking additional opportunities for exposure to coding has become more of a priority in some educational organizations. As we continue to seek opportunities for coding in school, it is more apparent that students are engaged when exposed to the power of programming languages. With coding, starting backward has proven to be a powerful strategy in demonstrating the value of this skill. For example, sharing statistics with parents and students that specify the demand for programmers and jobs in coding, taking students on field trips to high-tech work sharing spaces or coding camps, and even a simple task such as asking students to play the beloved game of Pacman and then asking them to consider how the game was created can all get their attention when it comes to the benefits of learning to code.

Going beyond the hour of code to build various coding activities into the maker experience is not only fun but simple to implement. Code.org has incredible unplugged activities that have proven to be popular even among our older students. Some of these activities include graph paper programming, learning about conditionals with a deck of cards by making up a card game that has a unique point system, or programming a human robot with simple written commands when no talking is aloud. Such activities that encourage movement and collaboration reinforce the concepts behind programming. If the goal is to use technology in the makerspace, the creators of Scratch have made this accessible for all ages. The free app ScratchJr gives even younger students the opportunity to create a powerful digital story using simple blocks in drag-and-drop programming. Alternatively, the Scratch Web site allows students program elaborate games that can become quite complex. Osmo has created a coding game that blends the tangible and the digital. Using actual coding blocks and placing them in front of the Osmo's front-facing camera, students can control what is happening on their screen. Practicing coding skills in this way helps students understand the relationship between coding and the real world.

Play-Doh: It Still Holds So Much Charm

All kids love Play-Doh. In the early days of iPads, I discovered a fun app called Play Dates with Play-Doh. The app provided step-by-step visuals for creating works of art made of Play-Doh. The library of objects one could create was extensive and could be tied into many themes that our younger students were studying. This made for a great Maker Monday project with the younger students, and, to enhance it with the older students, we also asked that they create stop-motion movies with their Play-Doh characters and objects. By differentiating the Maker Monday activity, the supplies were the same, but accommodations were made for different age levels and abilities. To date, there is a newer version of the Play-Doh app by Hasbro, called Play-Doh Touch Shape to Life. This free app incorporates virtual reality so that the Play-Doh creations

Play-Doh and iPads Come Together.

appear to come to life on the screen. After creating a character with Play-Doh, scanning the object with the iPad allows the character to enter a virtual world. Again, this is another means to help students consider the relationship between the tactile and the digital.

Digital Pottery

Maker activities that encourage thinking with the hands, teach the value of hard work, and also inspire creativity are meaningful makered projects. Digital pottery with the Let's Create! Pottery HD Lite app blends all of the goals. This free app allows makers to custom-design a piece of pottery, "sell" it in the online store to the highest bidder, and use the accumulated coins to purchase additional art supplies. Students are encouraged to create their own unique styles, understand the value of currency and financial literacy, and experience the drive to improve upon their work. Although students do not get to feel the clay between their fingers as they throw it onto the pottery wheel, they do get to appreciate the value of hard work—and without the mess. Requiring the students to sketch out their pottery design before creating the digital version encourages thoughtful planning and emphasizes the importance of a blueprint in the design process.

Meditative Maker Monday

We all need a time out from life every now and then. This realization was the inspiration behind Meditative Maker Monday. Students came to tap into their Zen side while also taking a break from technology. The art teacher at our school does a formal lesson on Zentangles so students are familiar with the concept prior to Meditative Maker Monday. Creating Zentangles is the practice of drawing in a structured pattern without planning ahead. There are suggested "rules" as to the size of the paper, and the preferred color choice is

Zentangles on Meditative #MakerMonday.

black. As stated in *Psychology Today*, Zentangles are meant to teach us to embrace mistakes and weave them into a creation as well as wander aimlessly (Malchiodi, 2014). It is a calming practice that we decided to enhance by dimming the lights and playing classical music. Not only did the students enjoy it, but the teachers wanted to get involved too.

A Cultural Revolution

While it started simply and gradually, maker education has changed our school culture. Due to the positive student feedback, the appreciation on the part of the parents, the earned support from the teachers, and the impact this has had on our administration in helping them to demonstrate the value of a school that is reflective and willing to grow and change, the momentum of the maker movement in our school has translated into significantly shaping our school culture. For instance, as part of our 2016 capital campaign, funds were raised to design and build an innovation and design studio and to outfit the studio with additional resources to further the maker culture. Now that the space has been completed, we have a state-of-art creation lab, as well as a new audio and visual production studio that is designed for moviemaking and audio projects. These new spaces have further enhanced the curricular connections between the media team, the core classroom teachers, and the other specialists. For example, our second-grade teachers now schedule an additional class period to extend the making beyond that of creating simple machines out of Legos. Now students also design their simple machines in Tinkercad's 3D software, have their designs judged by a Shark Tank–style panel, and earn the right to have their designs 3D-printed for usage in the classroom in conjunction with their simple machines unit.

As the maker culture has evolved, so has the need for additional support. As a result, we now have a team of students, known as the Network Sherpas, who are charged with being technology leaders within our school community. The Network Sherpas help facilitate Maker Mondays, coteach in the Innovation and Design Studio, support our teachers when technical difficulties arise, and present our innovative creations in front of a larger community as representatives of our school. Initially an opportunity for fifth graders, the Network Sherpa program, in its second year, now includes sixth and seventh graders, allowing further opportunities for older students to mentor the younger students while modeling appropriate technology usage. Additionally, the Network Sherpas are in the process of working with the middle school media specialist to develop a Tinkering Tuesday program on our middle school campus. Becoming a Network

Sherpa requires completing an online application, receiving teacher recommendations, and obtaining parent permission. Empowering the students through this program has become another attractive opportunity unique to the students in our school and born out of Maker Monday.

WHAT'S NOW AND WHAT'S NEXT

As we continue to gain financial, spatial, and personnel support for growing the maker culture in our school, we continue to revisit the current programming opportunities to help us cultivate designers, engineers, programmers, architects, artists, and entrepreneurs. Our school's media specialist recently launched an author podcast series in which students, working in teams, conduct research on our upcoming visiting authors, develop interview questions, and create unique podcasts to add to our growing author podcast series hosted on our Soundcloud channel. Our book clubs have joined forces with the Libraries as Incubator Project so that each student book club meeting now includes a mini-maker project that directly ties into the theme of the book. The Libraries as Incubator Project was created by three students in the Library and Information Studies program at the University of Wisconsin–Madison, whose mission is to demonstrate that libraries are places to connect and to create. We continue to grow our professional learning network through social media and face-to-face conferences, while also cultivating student leadership opportunities from within our own school so that we, too, can add to other educators' professional growth as it relates to maker education. We will continue to host innovative learning opportunities for our parents, grandparents, board members, other area schools, all of which are driven by our students' maker experiences. Inspiring other teachers continues to be a positive outcome as well. Our Judaics teacher has cultivated an entire curriculum out of Jewish-themed makered opportunities for third, fourth, and fifth graders. Unquestionably, students are more engaged, inspired, and invested in their Judiacs learning as a result of bridging makered and religious studies.

Having watched the maker education in our school start as a small seed and grow into a movement that has permeated so many other areas, I can only predict that the process of thinking with our hands will continue to extend to other subject areas as a critical part of the instruction. Students will ultimately come to expect a deep learning experience that allows them the space, the time, and the freedom to shape their learning in this way. Our mission statement explicitly states that children are encouraged to reach their highest potential and that our school's mission is to create a community in which children develop a lifelong love of learning. As stated in the Maker Movement Manifesto by Mark Hatch (2014), "Making is fundamental to what it means to be human. We must make, create, and express ourselves to feel whole. There is something unique about making physical things. These things are like little pieces of us and seem to embody portions of our souls." Developing a lifelong love of learning while striving to reach our highest potential is nothing short of nurturing the soul. It is this relationship between the Maker Manifesto and our school's mission that ensures we will continue to value the unique opportunities that making brings to the learning experience.

RECOMMENDATIONS

Based on our maker experiences, I would make three key points. First, start small. Prior to investing significant money, time, or planning, it is wise to start small in order to gauge the maker responsiveness on the part of your school community. For example, selecting one project, sharing the opportunity to participate, and selecting a project time that creates low stress for students, teachers, and the facilitator will help ease your school into the idea of a maker-oriented space. Second, pick something that invites passion on the part of the facilitator. If the maker facilitator is passionate about the project, that enthusiasm will transfer to the students. For example, I have a fascination with roller coasters, probably because I am quite scared of them. Putting together a brown bag of supplies, such as straws, rubber bands, tin foil, glue, and marbles and challenging students to design and create a roller coaster for their "marble" proved to be a meaningful maker project. Finally, I suggest revisiting your school's mission statement and consider how you can tie maker projects into your school's mission. Challenging students to design and build beyond their comfort zones motivates them to grow their knowledge base while reinforcing a love of learning.

CONCLUSIONS

Maker education benefits everyone. Students who struggle to sit still in class will find their place within the maker movement. The engagement level is significant and appeals to learners of all ages. It is no coincidence that there has been a surge in Escape Rooms for adults or the inclusion of Breakout EDU games for students. It is human nature to learn by doing. As stated by Martinez and Stager (2013), "Projects create memories for students" (p. 95). Be the educator who creates these opportunities for your students. Start making, even if it is just on a Monday.

REFERENCES

"4th Grade Technology." Blog. July 5, 2017. http://4techdavis.blogspot.com/

Hatch, Mark. *Maker Movement Manifesto*. New York: McGraw-Hill, 2014.

Malchiodi, Cathy. (2014). "Calm Down and Get Your Zentangle On." Blog. *Psychology Today*. June 30, 2017. https://www.psychologytoday.com/blog/arts-and-health/201403/calm-down-and-get-your-zentangle

Martinez, Sylvia Libow, and Gary S. Stager. *Invent to Learn*. Torrance, CA: Constructing Modern Knowledge Press, 2013.

MIT Media Lab. "Lego's Mindstorms." Blog. Massachusetts Institute of Technology, July 1, 2017. https://www.media.mit.edu/sponsorship/getting-value/collaborations/mindstorms

Wagner, Tony. *Creating Innovators: The Making of Young People Who Will Change the World*. New York: Scribner, 2012.

2

Wide Open Spaces: Creating a School Makerspace in an Open School

Stacy Hammer

INTRODUCTION

Libraries, including school libraries, are getting a facelift. Stuffy, quiet, dusty libraries filled with shushing and quiet reading are a thing of the past. To stay relevant, librarians have assessed the needs of their users and have changed the dynamics of the library to fit the needs of the community, school, and patrons. Some libraries turn to information and learning commons, study and collaboration cafés, mobile learning stations, or even flipped classrooms. Some libraries have turned to library makerspaces. As a new librarian, I inherited a unique library space in an open school with an open library. The library has two walls and is open to classrooms without barriers. Though the library space is unique, the previous library program was traditional. To set a new tone, build interest, and meet the needs of the library users, our makerspace began. A makerspace is an area of a library where materials and programming for building, creating, and inventing are available. Ours started small and simple. It has grown, had challenges, and continues to evolve. As part of that evolution, this year our open library is "opening its doors" (metaphorically—it is an open library, we do not have doors) to a partnership with a local college professor and the Friends of the Rappahannock to develop a Chesapeake Bay project. This project will offer more making opportunities to students and bring the real world into our library maker-space. This addition will create authentic opportunities to create, make, and solve real problems in our community.

RESEARCH IN THE FIELD

Research on open schools is extremely limited because open schools were a product of the 1970s education model, and most buildings that were originally built as open schools have been remodeled to support a more traditional class-room environment. That being said, the research does provide some interesting information about open schools and students' productivity in the library. Beeken and Janzen (1978) provided research that elementary school students in open schools spent more time in the school library than students in a traditional school because in most open schools, libraries are centrally located and close to classes. Some students are able to enter the library without being out of sight of the teacher. In the same study, it was concluded that they interact with other students more in an open school and have more opportunity for movement. The study also confirms the hypothesis that students are exposed to more activities and a larger assortment of learning materials. It was a sur-prise to see that research done almost 40 years ago supports the use of mak-erspaces in an open school. My library is centrally located, and students are able to easily pop into the library to check out a book, check in with me, or check into a making opportunity that provides a different way to learn.

The maker movement is not new in the sense that people have always been making things, but its recent introduction to the education setting is new. In some ways, it draws upon constructivist learning methods with learning through play, experimentation, and authentic inquiry. The effects of the movement can be seen both in higher education settings and in elementary schools: Students are learning by creating (Halverson & Sheridan, 2014). Adding a makerspace to a library can provide patrons access to learning opportunities they may not have elsewhere and at the same time shows that libraries are locations not just to absorb and gain information but also to create, imagine, and invent (Moorefield-Lang, 2015). School library makerspaces also fit in with AASL's *Standards for the 21st-Century Learner* in that they allow students to develop skills, dispositions, responsibilities, and strategies listed within the stan-dards (Canino-Fluit, 2014). With roots strong in education theory, practices supported by AASL's *21st-Century Standards*, and opportunities for students to access learning in an innovative way in our library, a makerspace seemed like a strong program to bring to my library.

MY MAKERSPACE STORY

Our makerspace is in the library. It has become a place for a whole lot of things to happen. Kids check out books. I teach lessons on subjects from research to digital citizenship and add love of reading along the way. The library is centrally located, and almost all the visitors to the school must pass by the library on their way to their destinations. As a library student at Longwood University, I had learned about the makerspace movement but had not observed one in the library. Makerspaces seemed like a good fit for a middle school or high school, but with a fixed schedule and a unique library space, I was unsure how to make it happen. That said, I felt compelled to bring making to the library in some form. I knew I needed to change the traditional perception of the library because I believe school libraries can be a vibrant hub of learning where students have access to materials and opportunities. I added maker opportunities from the start. They were informal. They were small. It began to change the way students and teachers viewed the library.

SET UP CENTERS, AND THEY WILL COME

I started with ideas so small, they seemed almost insignificant. The previous class routine in my library consisted of a library lesson and checkout time; then students found a place to read until their teacher came to get them. To give students more choice, I added centers as an option after they checked out books. The first change I observed was that students chose their books and checked them out with a purpose. Students stopped feigning interest in books to buy time before the end of library. Rather, students moved about the library with their goal in mind and immediately claimed their spot at a center. These centers were not highly technical. Nor were there great directions or goals. There were problems to solve to make it run smoothly, but it was a start. Sometimes, a start is all one needs to move in the right direction. Center options included:

- Bookmark making.
- Drawing books with paper and colored pencils.
- Jenga.
- Word games.
- Puzzles.

At this point, I would not say I had a makerspace. What I did have was a change in what library users expected to see in the library. I made a list of my goals and considered how to achieve them. I also talked to anyone who would listen about makerspaces and the use of making and technology in the library. I shared my plan with my principal both on paper and in meetings. I met with the school's parent–teacher organization not to ask for anything in particular but to share my plan. I worked closely with the school technology resource teacher and the gifted resource teacher.

MAKE FRIENDS

My class schedule is fixed, which means I see classes all day in 45-minute sessions. While I teach a class of kids, the teacher is collaborating with her or his grade level. This did not leave me many opportunities to meet with classroom teachers or even to find ways to incorporate makerspace into daily lessons. I was a first-year librarian and new to navigating elementary schools. I met the school's gifted teacher, a teacher who specializes in meeting the educational needs of students who have the potential talent to perform above average, and she was already very invested in bringing Science, Technology, Engineering, Art, and Math (STEAM) to all students in our school. We both viewed STEAM as something all students should experience. Together, we started an after-school club for students. Students in grades three through five signed up to participate in design challenges. They were given materials, a scenario, and a goal. Students worked collaboratively to solve the problem and build together. It was very important to me that all students had the opportunity to participate. Students from all achievement levels participated and benefited from our club, affectionately titled, Maker Monday. We built catapults, made Lego® mosaics, built towers using toothpicks and gumdrops. Again, it was not fancy, but Maker Monday happened in the library. Students, teachers, and parents began to see the library differently.

SUPPORT AND ADVOCACY

I shared what was happening in the library with anyone who would listen. Though some saw what was happening simply as an opportunity for kids to play with toys, others began to support us. The county in which I work began an Elementary School Makerspace Initiative where a few libraries were granted some makerspace materials. Our school was lucky enough to be included. We received a 3D printer, several sets of snap circuits (a battery-powered kit where students can practice making closed circuits by snapping lights and motors to the power source), and several sets of Makey Makeys® (an invention kit that allows makers to turn everyday objects into touch pads). These tools added to our after-school program and allowed me more opportunities by adding making to centers with students. Through my work with the makerspace grant, I was also introduced to a professor from Mary Washington University, Dr. George Meadows. Dr. Meadows has worked with school and public libraries to build makerspaces and has supported our program in many ways. He visited the library to see what we were doing. He invited me to his campus to see and learn from his makerspace at Mary Washington University and continues to be a great supporter of our library program.

I ended my first year as a school librarian with support, ideas, success, failure, and many more supplies. Dr. Meadows endowed building tools, coding tools, and additional supplies. I added building pieces with scholastic money from the book fair. At times I was not sure if continuing to build a makerspace was the right path for me to follow, but the universe has a funny way of pulling you in the direction you need to go.

MOVING FORWARD IN YEAR TWO

Going into my second year as a librarian, I had many more resources available and a little more experience than the year before. I continued with centers but changed them up. They became more technical, and there was more

Makerspace Check in Sheet

Student Names	Teacher

Start Time	Proposed Product

Materials You Need	Plan

Drawing

Maker Planning Sheets.

structure to them. Students now had opportunities to complete planning sheets before building in a center and had a reflection sheet (see figure) to consider what could be done differently in the future.

Some centers include:

- *Bookmark making*—Students use paper, coloring utensils, scissors, glue, stamps, and paper punches to design and create a bookmark. These can be free choice or follow a design challenge, such as to create a bookmark that represents the book you are reading or create a bookmark that celebrates Read across America Week.
- *STEAM bins*—I have several boxes available for students with an assortment of building tools available. There are boxes with blocks, index cards and tape, Popsicle® sticks with rubber bands, pipe cleaners, and more. The options are endless. Students choose a box, then select a card from a bucket. The card has a picture or text directions on what to build. Since the boxes and the cards are interchangeable, the number of building options is endless. Students are able to write planning sheets and reflection sheets. These centers are also great to switch in and out and can be adapted seasonally.
- *Lego bins*—A bin of Legos is available along with a building challenge. I change the challenge out each month.
- *Snap circuits*—Students use snap circuits to build and tinker. Some follow the direction booklet; other choose to create on their own. I have also written some challenges for students to try.
- *Ozobots*—The Ozobot® center allows students to practice coding with the mini robot and markers. The Ozobot Web site has some wonderful resources to scaffold learning.
- *Robotic mouse*—The mouse is programmed to navigate a labyrinth students build. I have also created mats connected to Math and Language Arts curriculum for the mouse to navigate. For sight word coding (great for kindergarten and first grade), students pull a sight word from a box, read it aloud, find it on the mat, and program the mouse to move to the word. For number coding (appropriate for any elementary grade depending on the math problem), students pull a math problem from a box, solve the problem, find the answer on the mat, and code the mouse to move to the answer. This is a great opportunity to practice coding that is appropriate for the youngest students.

The evolution of the centers has allowed students more time to tinker with tools that are both low tech and high tech. Many of the high-tech centers pull science and computer science skills into library time.

MAKING AND READING

Though the centers were a wonderful place to start and will probably always be a part of my library, I wanted to move to a place where the idea of making was a part of library lessons. Making is wonderful, but, as a librarian and the cheerleader for reading in the building, I grappled with where reading fits in. I did not want to ignore stories as I moved toward making. To incorporate both, I began using design briefs in lessons for students, when appropriate. A design brief challenged students to create something, usually to solve a problem, using specific criteria. I found that by my starting with a story, students have access to literature and can then build and create to solve a problem. I get some designs from the Virginia Department of Education Web site; others I write myself. Students work in small groups to discuss, plan, build, question, and sometimes find success. I basically follow this format:

Number Coding with a Robotic Mouse.

1. *Read the story*—Many stories provide great problems or challenges that can be used as a starting point for a design challenge. As a librarian, I feel it is important to have design challenges begin with a story. Sometimes I even work in some research so that students must use a variety of resources available in the library.
2. *Identify a problem or product* connected to the story.
3. *Set up the criteria*—Setting up the criteria really depends on the task at hand. Some great ideas to consider include the object must have a moving part, it must hold something, or it must be able to move something.
4. *Time limit*—Considering that I have a 45-minute class period and students need time to check out library books, I usually spread a design challenge over two weeks. In week one, I read the story, students may do some research, and they may write a plan. On day two, students have about 20 minutes to complete their design. If I assign a more advanced design, I give students more time and add another week to our timetable.
5. *Material limit*—Kids can be so wasteful! Some ideas to keep students aware of what they are using include assigning costs to each item and giving them a budget, allowing students to choose a certain number of items from each basket, or assigning a specific list of materials to each group.
6. *Time to make*—Last, I give them time to make. Students problem-solve, discuss, sometimes argue, feel success and failure. Sometimes students do not accomplish the goal within the allotted time. It can be hard for kids to accept that, but the library makerspace is a great spot

for elementary kids to experience a little bit of failure. They learn they can bounce back and try again next time. It promotes a growth mindset, and kids benefit greatly from it.

7. *Reflect*—When time allows, it is beneficial for students to complete a reflection sheet. Topics on the sheet can include the group's strengths, weaknesses, team member contributions, and what they would do differently if given a chance to complete a design challenge again.

This has been a fantastic way to incorporate making into the daily library class. Students are engaged in both the love of story and the problem solving of building. Here is a quick example of this type of activity. I read the picture book *The Snatchabook* by Helen and Thomas Docherty to students. We discuss the characters and the problem. We identify that the Snatchabook was stealing books, so the students will make a trap to catch the critter. I set up criteria, such as the trap must hold a small stuffed animal, and it must not hurt the Snatchabook. I could make the project more complex by requiring a pulley system or such. I review the available material, which includes cardboard from tissue boxes, tape, pipe cleaners, and the like. Students have 20 minutes to build the trap; then they can present it either to the whole group or within small groups.

I AM NOT SMARTER THAN A FIFTH GRADER

I found that I had many awesome tools and that I knew very little about them. I admit that many of the things our library received I felt more than a little intimidated to use. To overcome the fear, I created a project for fifth graders. The library hosted a month of making. In that month, all the kits and tools were available to try out during library time. Students tried them out. I was honest with them when I did not know how to use some of the kits, and sometimes I helped them figure them out. Sometimes they figured out the kits without me. At the end of the month, kids wrote a review of the products and

Makings for a Robotic Arm.

submitted their opinion of the tools via Google Classroom. Now students have a much better understanding of the tools we have and how to use them. Each student is not an expert at everything, but every class has at least one expert with each tool and is called upon to teach others . . . including me sometimes.

Truthfully, after the month of making, I feel more comfortable with more of the tools. Most important, students are now ready to use the tools to create projects in conjunction with library research and learning. Most importantly, I have fifth graders who more connected to the library than they have ever been. Students now ask to come in during lunch to work on building a robotic arm. It is not a grade. It is not an assignment. It is something they started on their own, and, working in 20-minute time slots, they continue to chip away at the project. They have shown me perseverance, responsibility, grit, and pride in their work. This opportunity would not have been available without our school makerspace.

CHESAPEAKE BAY PROJECT

Our next big project is working with the Friends of the Rappahannock on a Chesapeake Bay project. Founded in 1985, the Friends of the Rappahannock has provided advocacy, restoration, and education to preserve our local waterways. The Friends of the Rappahannock education department has created design challenges for schools to use to continue the education. Through a grant, I have been able to be a part of this wonderful project. Educators from the Friends of the Rappahannock met with a few librarians and teachers to train us, and the group is providing resources to create design challenges for students to participate in. One challenge describes a pollution problem: Litter is falling into the storm drains. Design a filter that will prevent litter and pollution to enter the water and polluting the Chesapeake Bay watershed. We will read stories connected to pollution, research possible solutions, then build

designs to solve the problem. It is exciting to bring real-world problems into our library space. Students can now actually apply their learning to something that affects our local area, the Chesapeake Bay watershed.

THE POWER OF YES

In my makerspace journey, simply saying yes has provided me with more opportunities than anything else. Saying yes to trying something different in my library space changed the library experience for many kids. Saying yes to working with others gave me chances to learn from their experience and to share what I know. Saying yes to accepting the grant

Filter Designs for Watershed Project.

from the county and from Mary Washington allowed for so many opportunities, even though I felt I was less than worthy. I said yes to makerspaces, even when I was unsure of what the role of a school librarian is in the makerspace world.

LOOKING TO THE FUTURE

I see a great value in project-based learning opportunities that combine making in the library, but to fully develop projects, collaborating with classroom teachers is key. Providing access in the library is perfect, but it is more meaningful instruction when students see a clear connection to their classroom instruction. It is also imperative that I keep story alive. Any design challenge should involve stories and research in order to create a well-rounded learning experience.

Even though they are informal, I plan to never lose the centers. That chance for building time with no stakes is an important part of the library makerspace idea. Little unstructured tinker time is available for students, and developmentally that is an important activity for young people.

THINKING ABOUT STARTING A LIBRARY MAKERSPACE?

So you are thinking about starting a makerspace in your school library. Do it! Here are some tips I learned along the way:

- *Start small*—If I tried to change everything in a week, things would have gone wrong, and I would have felt discouraged. Do not do that to yourself! Try one thing at a time, and celebrate the small successes. Your first project does not need to include 3D printing. That is a big endeavor that requires time and background knowledge. Instead, start with what you have and with what you feel comfortable using. Kids may find making and design challenges frustrating at first. Remember, change takes time. Try small projects, see the results, and plan another from there. Within no time, you will realize you have a space buzzing with makers.
- *Do not be intimidated by things you know little about*—I have found that once kids have the free time to figure something out, they usually do. I admit when I am not sure how to do something and have not lost a bit of credibility with my students. In fact, they love to help me, and their helping has probably improved my relationships with them.
- *Make the stuff you get accessible*—It does no good to have a set of Ozobots and never use them. It took me some time to accept this. I was afraid the pieces would get lost or broken. In the end, I have to trust in the rules and procedures, and, most importantly, I must trust in my kids.
- *Be willing to find a new way*—For a good six months, I was determined to build a Lego wall in the library. They are so cool. I could never make

the commitment to do it. During class one day, a student was using some magnetic building blocks. The student stuck one to our metal wall. It stuck. It was like a lightbulb went off in my head. We didn't need a Lego wall when we had a magnet wall! I set up a center for students to build on the wall using the magnetic blocks. It has proved to be a success from kindergarten to

Shapes on Our Magnetic Wall.

fifth grade. I did not think of it on my own. A third grader showed me because third graders are not afraid to try new things.

CONCLUSION

Makerspaces may be a fad, much like the open concept school. Even if that is the case, once the fad is done and gone, the benefits of makerspaces can live on. Hands-on, collaborative learning, creating, access to books, and technology—these things will likely always be what kids need and can be provided by a school librarian.

REFERENCES

Beeken, Don, and Henry L. Janzen. "Behavioral Mapping of Student Activity in Open-Area and Traditional Schools." *American Educational Research Journal 15*, no. 4 (1978): 507–517.

Canino-Fluit, Ana. "School Library Maker Spaces: Making It Up as I Go." *Teacher Librarian 41*, no. 5 (2014): 21.

Halverson, Erica Rosenfeld, and Kimberly Sheridan. "The Maker Movement in Education." *Harvard Educational Review 84*, no. 4 (2014): 495–504.

Moorefield-Lang, Heather. "Making, Libraries, and Literacies." *Library Media Connection 33*, no. 4 (2015): 30–31.

Part II

Middle Grades

3

Makers Gonna Make

IdaMae Craddock

INTRODUCTION

Making. Making is not electronics, or crafts, or wood shop, or robotics, or any one item. Rather, it is a way of thinking about the world and a way to teach students life skills that are not always explicitly laid out in state standards. Making is a way for students to learn the concept of failing up, to practice creative problem solving, and to become adept at online research. Making is a way to approach learning and instructional design.

Persisting through failure is a core concept of the maker movement. In middle school, students have not yet lost the magic of their imagination and, as a result, aren't so stuck in the box created by what we engage in through our adult experiences. Solutions that, as adults, we may dismiss are not out of the realm of the imaginations of youth. Creative problem solving is a normal part of childhood that is forced into obsolescence by the pervasiveness of the "right" answers in schools. Embedded maker education in schools is a chance for students to use their creativity to learn that not every answer is binary in nature. Building, creating, and exploring without the quest for correctness simply are not offered enough in our schools. Maker education is the opportunity to practice creatively by working through problems as adults do—without a correct answer looming.

The great thinkers of our time—Steve Jobs, Elon Musk, Cynthia Breazeal—all are epic failures. Have you ever heard of Macintosh TV? The Apple LISA? The Apple III? The Power Mac g4 Cube? Probably not. They were all failures. However, Macintosh TV is now the wildly popular Apple TV; the LISA introduced a graphical user interface that is now the basis of all computer operating systems. Failures were merely the building blocks for the next iteration. The technology in our iPhones has its roots in the G4 Cube. Without those failures and their inventors' persistence to move past them, progress would not have been possible. The process of ideation, creation, failure, and iteration that is endemic to making mimics the concept of building successes upon failures. In the pedagogy of maker education, students have an idea, build it, likely watch it not work, and keep trying. The view of failure not as a stopping point but as a stepping-stone is a life skill by which students can learn from their mistakes—really pointing toward the soft skill of persistence (Kurti, Kurti, & Fleming, 2014).

Finding answers is a skill embedded in maker education. Knowing what to ask of whom, how, and where is a research skill that makes up the foundation of libraries since the beginning of time. Maker education allows these skills to meet with and fuel a new interest in entrepreneurial and communication needs in a natural way.

In addition to the social awkwardness that makes middle schoolers so endearing, they still are working outside the box. Developmentally, middle schoolers are so ready for creativity. According to G. J. Smith, "As we follow the spiral upwards from the age of 5 we again encounter a phase of subjective expansion around the age of 10–11, but an expansion at a higher level of cognitive sophistication, less dependent on accidental impressions and more on material incorporated into the child's private self" (Smith & Carlsson, 1983, p. 24). Middle school students are in a unique state in which they are developing creatively and incorporating new information into their cognitive schema. In addition, teaching creative problem solving in early adolescence is effective in the long term (Baer, 1988). This makes a strong case for teaching through making and using the maker mindset in the middle school, as it will have a lasting effect on their abilities to problem solve, research, and create interesting solutions.

LITERATURE

Middle school making must take advantage of the unique opportunities afforded by middle schooler's creativity by hitting the sweet spot between design thinking, project-based learning (PBL), and research. A large sample size in a 2008 study by Mehalik and colleagues compared scripted inquiry to design thinking and found that "a systems design approach for teaching science concepts has superior performance in terms of knowledge gain achievements, engagement, and retention when compared with a guided inquiry approach" (Mehalik et al., 2008, p. 80). Most literature on design thinking is confined to math and science; my own experience supports the finding that instruction based in design thinking and maker education results in gains in subject knowledge, engagement, and retention. For teachers, design thinking pushes us to help students with questions that have not yet been addressed in the academic or practitioner literature. For students, there is tremendous value in creating their own paradigms to find and sort information and to create meaning as their projects progress.

However, in order to make the gains promised by the Mehalik et al. study (2008), maker education must incorporate aspects of design thinking into instruction. As librarians and instructional leaders, we are uniquely able to make connections among math, science, language arts, and history. Getting students and teachers to incorporate making across subjects requires not just tools or a space but an environment that is safe in a variety of ways, that is carefully crafted to start conversations, and that is present and accessible.

FIRST STEPS

I know that most library transformations begin with a good weed, but the story of Jackson P. Burley Middle School's library transformation did not start that way. It began with buzzers. Made of faux wood paneling and giant aluminum tubing, these antitheft sensors made the library not so welcoming. They stand on either side of the entrance and loudly beep at anyone who dares pass through with an item that belongs to the library. Punishing, embarrassing, or even drawing attention to middle school students is a recipe for them never to come back.

I decided they had to go. As I was hacking away at them, the science teacher stopped in to introduce himself and lend a hacksaw and later a dremel to the cause. He did ask why I was taking out my stress on these buzzers. My honest answer was that students should not be nervous about checking out books and equipment from the library. It is their library. All of it ultimately belongs to the school community. Middle school students have such high social anxiety that the fear of being singled out is often enough to make them decide it would be better off not to come in—much less check anything out. The buzzers were the first to go.

The next step continues to pay significant dividends two years later. I opened the doors. Both front and back doors are now unlocked, and the front doors are propped open. Open doors make it easy to stop by or check out a display. The whole school community now feels welcome to cut through, play a move on the community chess board, or color something. The message is to come see what's happening or ask a quick question. You don't have to commit a serious amount of time.

Truly open access also means that the profoundly disabled students are now in the library, sometimes multiple times a day. Ms. R and her assistant Ms. B had not visited the library for some time, but now they feel welcome and bring students. Small daily interactions have led to their students dusting, tidying, and maintaining the beautiful window garden they created. All students should have access to making, and the content area teachers are one of those keys. Ms. R has found a way for her students to access a maker curriculum in a small way because I unlocked the door closest to her classroom.

WORKING WITH THE SPACE

Transforming a library is a delicate process, and the politics surrounding it can be tricky. My first roadblock that first summer came after I took down the circulation desk. Where, they asked, were we supposed to put the food for faculty meetings? I suggested a folding table, and that appeared to be an acceptable alternative when covered with a tablecloth. My explanation to teachers: the space was needed for students to work.

Responding to changes in the library with an acceptable alternative, paired with a student-centered, access-driven explanation, seems to calm the fear of change that affects both students and teachers. Knowing that I am not taking a sledgehammer to the circulation desk just because I am having a bad day but rather because I have self-checkout set up at a smaller location and the space is going to be used for student-centered making activities has helped smooth the way. Such a twin offering is very powerful in creating a sense of safety. It is reassurance that the changes are not random but rather carefully crafted for specific purposes.

I knew the layout of the library was not moving toward openness. More of a fortress than an invitation, the circulation desk did not communicate welcome. It was a barrier and not a workbench—both metaphorically and literally. It blocked the entrance to the library office, which was shortly to become the makerspace.

Offering a variety of spaces is important to create that sense of comfort and safety. Encouraging students must ultimately move past passive welcoming and into creation. From me, that means active, verbal permission: saying yes. For example, Ben is a sixth-grade student. When new Hummingbird boards (part of a customizable robot kit) came in, he came to ask if he could see one. Since I had not had a chance to try them yet, I told him yes—to take the kit and see what he could make. Another teacher added that he should be careful, that he might break it, and that he should stay at a table because he will probably lose one of the pieces. Just watching his shoulders descend from proud to uncertain was heartbreaking. I handed the Hummingbird to a now reluctant Ben and told him that it would be fine, that he was smart and great at robotics, and that he would make something amazing—which he did. Thirty minutes later, he had a working decibel meter. That is the power of yes in a maker library.

Get out of the way when students want to learn. What we perceive to be care for the equipment ends up not only not protecting the equipment but also stifling the learning. In a maker library, I want both students and faculty to walk in and feel comfortable enough that they will pick up something interesting—whether it is a book or a robot or a pile of cardboard or a new instructional strategy and try it. If it fails, so be it. I hope that a fail will be a fail up.

MOVING TOWARD MAKING

Keeping the learning right in front as a goal makes a lot of the changes much easier. The mantra "what's best for kids" is not a mere slogan but a guiding principle. It drives everything from where the duct tape is stored to which instructional strategies I am going to attempt. Articulating the mission in a short group of words in a powerful way opens doors among faculty and staff. "What is best for kids?" is a great question to ask in any meeting. Whether it is discussing a system for allowing access to the library or figuring out how many classes can be in the library at once, it is a wonderful question to use in faculty meetings of any size. It redirects the conversation in a profound way.

Invited to speak on the National Public Radio last year about the move toward project-based and passion-based learning in a maker library, I was asked, "Why? Isn't it much harder to teach this way?" Of course it is. My answer was clear: "It's what's best for kids." The easy way and the best way are not always the same thing. PBL offers engagement and retention far exceeding both scripted inquiry (Mehalik et al., 2008, p. 80) and traditional instruction (Hernández-Ramos, 2009). I spend approximately 75% of my day teaching collaboratively. Helping teachers by giving them strategies and offering to actually teach and assess with them create an environment of safe risk taking. Often, they are willing to make the shift if they do not have to do it alone.

MAKING AS A COMPONENT OF INSTRUCTION

The American Association of School Librarians mission statement is: "*The American Association of School Librarians empowers leaders to transform teaching and learning.*" We are empowered, as librarians, to transform teaching and learning. I stand very firm on the mission statement. School librarians are here to transform. I will ask "What's best for kids?" and then I will use it as a statement when explanations are called for. Finding your mission phrase is important when explaining to the staff why you are making changes. Let us return to the horrified reaction to the circulation desk. By having my mission phrase as a script, I could effectively explain how having more space to work, read, teach, and learn was best for kids. It is quite the handy phrase because having the faculty on board is critical to the success of the maker library.

You will need the support of the faculty to transform not only the learning but also the teaching. In addition to making the space accessible, I also had to make myself accessible. To do that, I left the library. Because the library was empty when I first arrived, I was able to go to *all* the meetings. It felt as though I had signed up for every committee on earth. Hospitality: yes. Team leaders: yes. Diversity: definitely. Technology: also definitely. I attended both subject area meetings and grade-level team meetings. I tried to be in many places, and I had a bit of a script that I would use to articulate services.

One favorite tip I learned from improv class is "yes, and." Mr. E, a fantastic language arts teacher at Burley, came in and asked if I had a microphone he could borrow. I said, "Yes, and . . . are you all doing recordings? Do you know that we have Audacity on the 1:1 laptops? I'd be happy to work with your class so that they know how to use it." Now I had a tech-rich project and could help with the instruction. That project has blossomed into a drama unit in which the students learn about sound by Skyping with a Foley artist, research the advertisements of the era, record the plays, and publish them to e-portfolios.

Math is a great example of a content area whose teachers sometimes have trouble viewing themselves in partnership with the school librarians. However, in two years, 63% of our math teachers have used the library for projects more than four times a year. Mr. C is a great math teacher but, by his own admission, knows little about coding. In Virginia, the state is preparing to mandate the teaching of coding in math classes. By attending the math department meeting, I get to use another of my favorite scripts, "Wouldn't it be fun if. . . ." The suggestion helps to transform a cause of stress—mandated coding—into something enjoyable. Mr. C and his entire professional learning community now do an open-ended choice coding project in the library every Friday for the entire second semester. We pair the library's research skills with the content area teachers' logical, sequential skills to assist the students in creating amazing coded projects.

I have also offered up whole lesson plans but never with the intent for them to be taught as is. I can't. The content area teacher knows the content, the class, and the timeline better than I ever can or will. In my first year with the school, I paired with a sixth-grade math teacher to do a project about area. I had a lesson plan for students to build a house, measure, calculate area, and then use their research skills to price a house. However, she knew her students needed fewer problems and a chance to really dream. The Dream Room project allotted an entire class period for the students to imagine and draw the most amazing bedroom they could envision. It was not until the next day that students started to talk about scale and measuring. It was two days before we began calculating and researching. She knew her students. While the lesson plan I offered was a great place to jump off, it was not the right thing. Respecting the expertise of the teacher in offering an encased plan is very important.

Transforming teaching and learning absolutely involves teaching outside our content area. Information literacy is embedded in every project and lesson presented. I have taught everything from genomic classification to Spanish with information literacy skills embedded. Making is exactly the same way. Make "making" no big deal. Just add it to the lesson like any other strategy.

Mr. S was one of the first teachers to approach me to work together last year. The project was Westward Expansion. The students researched a significant event in pairs and were provided search terms and a rating scale but not links because, as the librarian, I was pointing toward source evaluation as a skill. Then they were given red and green pieces of construction cardstock. First, they had to determine whether this was a positive event (green) or negative event (red) from the perspective of the Native American population and put the date and a short summary on the paper. I also provided scissors and tape. The students shortly began asking if they could combine the two colors. "Yes!" Having the students hang their cards toward the end of the lesson easily showed how the timeline grew increasingly negative. It was a very short and tight maker activity embedded in a history lesson. Ultimately, for the teacher, it was no big deal. Embedding maker education in the content becomes another instructional strategy in our collection of tools.

Making, whether its representations of knowledge, as in this case, or the quest to find knowledge, as in Mr. C's class, paid big dividends in retention, engagement, and acquisition of knowledge. But we as librarians can help transform the teaching by making it far less intimidating—casually embedding it in every lesson and every unit we have the opportunity to teach. We provide the opportunity for professional development that teachers need to make the pivot.

Spanish class is a great example of a class moving toward project-based learning. The students into the library to make pop-up books in Spanish.

During the first block, I showed the students examples, helped them cut and glue and paste, translated, and so on. By the last block, the students had it down. The teacher made more examples of different type of folds, knew how to orient the pages to pop up, and, *por supuesto*, knew the Spanish. This type of professional development happens in the moment; it is immediately pertinent, applicable, and durable. Three blocks later, the Spanish teacher is the master paper engineer, and I was the tape and glue fetcher. This year, we repeated the project with a controlled vocabulary lesson. Something else happened that I felt was important in creating that collegial relationship. The principal stopped in to ask a question. I looked at the teacher and then kept on teaching. The principal then said he would come back later. The teacher saw that I prioritized his class over administrative tasks. Students see you put the learning first, and that builds confidence in their making.

In advocating that librarians teach outside information literacy, I understand and live daily the fact that we cannot possibly know everything. What we do know is whom to call and/or where to look. I don't know all the answers, but I probably know someone who does.

My dad, for example. We were engaged in a project in which students imagined the school of the future. What it would look like, how learning would happen, how the building would be shaped and powered. I know next to nothing about building engineering and what is involved in LEED certifying a building, but I know who does. We Skyped twice with my dad, who spent 25 years as a building services manager. He was happy to evaluate the design, add information, and point them in appropriate directions for their research. In transforming teaching and learning, we also need to stretch and learn our own craft. Tapping resources is what we do, and we, probably more than any other content area in the school, are lifelong learners. While I had to give the poor students a blank look when they first asked about LEED certification, I now know that triple-pane windows are a must, as is a solid waste recycling program. It is scary to step outside the comfort zone, just as our content area teachers are when they engage in maker pedagogy. But teaching collaboratively means that there are (at least) two minds and four hands to do the work.

INDEPENDENT STUDENT MAKING

Middle school students have a freshness of perspective and the natural curiosity of childhood that has not yet been completely eroded by Sisyphean piles of worksheet packets. Several strategies engage students in untrammeled making.

Direct instruction and project-based learning get your foot in the door in helping students engage in making. Often they will learn how to operate a tool in a class and come back later with a good idea. For example, Kai and Demetrius started a recycled art project with the art teacher and me. After learning to use the sewing machine, they wondered aloud if Doritos® bags could be sewn. We tried. They could. They started construction of the sparkliest Mylar® suit jacket ever seen. What started small with a bit of instruction on how to work a basic sewing machine had blossomed into students making independently.

Exposure during class time is one way to show students how to engage in making, but once students are in the library, there are a myriad of options. One is to engage students in a simple make. Coloring is an amazing craft-ish community art project. Students come in, color for a bit, and walk away. It was wonderful during Standards of Learning testing because it is so relaxing. However, as often is the case with teenagers and relaxing activities, boredom will take up residence. Now, introducing new materials like obi tape, stamps, and origami keeps their interests and builds their capacity for making items. Piquing interest is one thing, but keeping it is quite another.

Alexandra started off as a colorer. She would stop in to color this and that. Soon she began using different materials to make coloring pages. Then she started with origami. Next was duct tape. Then sewing. Then sewing machine repair. Then sewing instruction. There is a path from small expressions of creativity to leadership through making. She felt safe to indulge her boredom with the next level of risk. Would she be reprimanded for using too much tape? Probably not. Would she get in trouble for using tools on the sewing machine? Also probably not. Would she be shushed when two other girls were with her at the sewing machine talking? No to that too. A comfortable environment where she feels safe from reprimand, even failure, led to not only skill building but also to research skills to fix the machine and social skills in leading other students into making.

What if she had broken the sewing machine? Making and Maker Education are a powerful way to teach research. When we protect the equipment, we often throw up a barrier to learning research. Alexandra learned all about tension and different thread weights in attempting to sew a fine lightweight knit with upholstery thread. If I had told her to stop using it, if I had sent it off for repair, if I had just told her the information, she would not have learned how to pair thread and fabric weights or how to find that information. As librarians, our content is mostly the how of learning. In letting students muddle their way through a maker project and providing resources, search terms, and reliable sources from time to time, we support the how.

By putting the emphasis on the content learned instead of the final product, we give permission to fail. I learned very early on in my teaching career that when demonstrating a project, it should fail "just enough." Each week, I set out a maker activity as passive programming. These offerings include Harry Potter wands, duct tape wallets, and origami Pikachu. In each case, I make an example that does not quite work. Perfection in examples drives perfection in the students. If I set out a perfectly done duct tape wallet, there is no room for students to improve the design. Why would they add a pocket if they weren't looking at the example to figure out why mine was crooked? Why would they eliminate the divider if they were not looking to see why mine wrinkled on the front?

Making a slightly terrible model pays exponential dividends in student creativity. It also legitimizes the concept of failing up. If I keep working on my wallet over a few days, they can see qualities like persistence, research, investigation, and even physics. I will walk up and fiddle with it while I talk to students. I give away terrible versions and start over. I ask students for advice, look up videos of wallet making, and unmake in order to remake. These are all pieces of the research process. I publicly acknowledge failed iterations and move on. All for legitimizing the learning process over the final product.

FINAL THOUGHTS

Making teaches students skills that are not in the curriculum but that are essential for success in the information age. The summative assessment of content learned is a traditional and oft cited way to measure knowledge gains in the content area. However, because making often results in iteration instead of completion, it is difficult to say when it is over. By grading the process of learning rather than the product, the impulse for students to stop working on a project when it meets the requirement is removed.

Often, as a classroom teacher, I had students ask what they needed to get an A. Making eliminates the ceiling and rewards the qualities we truly hope to see in our learners: persistence beyond failure, comfort with research, and interest in authentic and creative problem solving. These are all qualities measured by standardized tests—so we must find a way for students to learn them. Maker Education is a way to transform the teaching and learning in our schools in order to best position our students to succeed in a global economy.

LOOKING FORWARD

Having a maker library involves a lot of stuff. To quote Karen Muller, "It makes a lot of sense to provide our community with all manner of items to help them learn new skills and discover their world" (Muller, 2015, p. 26). While the movement toward a library of things began in the public libraries, school libraries also want to help students "learn new skills and discover their world." In the Information Age, the world is not necessarily contained in a book, nor is the world we see now the world for which we would like students to be prepared. Moore's law is in full effect in education. What they know now will be obsolete in three years, and that timeline is exponentially shrinking.

Henry, a graduate of Monticello High School, recently posted about the automata that they were making in his sophomore engineering class at the university. As I looked at it, I thought how similar it was to the automata being taught in my middle school's engineering exploratory class. I was shocked to learn that I should teach the same coding lesson to the sixth graders as I taught to the eighth graders earlier in the year. When we talk about what to teach in the realm of technology, we need to shift toward teaching students to think, not do. Having a library of things allows students to interact with and discover the world in a safe place. They are not learning what but rather how, and that is much more powerful. It builds research skills, thinking skills, and the concept of failing up.

However, having a rich library of things involves a lot of mess and necessitates a level of organization that is beyond what a school library may be prepared for. I, certainly, was unprepared for the level of organization required and years later still cannot pretend to know where everything is at all times. I can acknowledge that I will never be Pinterest worthy, but making is messy, and managing the chaos is an area of growth. Getting better at storing, tracking, and managing my library of things is an obstacle overcome with Tupperware and time—and both are in short supply. Time especially. Managing that time is a goal as I look forward, but it cannot drive the program.

Accommodations can be made to library procedures in order to better use time. Self-checkout is a great example. Checking out a walk-in patron, answering the phone, and dealing with broken laptops are all important tasks; however, they can be accomplished through agency. Students can check out their own books and loaner laptops. They can answer the phone. So having the librarian walk away from students who are learning in order to answer the phone is not acceptable. However, creating a community in which students have agency helps to allocate more time to the most important use of time—learning.

The American Library Association lays out our values very clearly. Time management is not a value. Access is, as are education and lifelong learning, diversity, and democracy. It is on those values that we would like to base a strong maker-oriented program. Relying on best practices grounded in research, engaging with classroom teachers as much as they will allow, and providing access to information, ideas, and inspiration to the community are all the hope of my program. For my school community, I would like to stand at the intersection of information, ideas, and inspiration.

REFERENCES

Baer, John M. "Long-Term Effects of Creativity Training with Middle School Students." *The Journal of Early Adolescence 8*, no. 2 (1988): 183–193.

Hernández-Ramos, Pedro, and Susan De La Paz. "Learning History in Middle School by Designing Multimedia in a Project-Based Learning Experience." *Journal of Research on Technology in Education 42*, no. 2 (2009): 151–173.

Kurti, R. Steven, Debby L. Kurti, and Laura Fleming. "The Philosophy of Educational Makerspaces Part 1 of Making an Educational Makerspace." *Teacher Librarian 41*, no. 5 (2014): 8–11.

Mehalik, Matthew M., Yaron Doppelt, and Christian D. Schuun. "Middle-School Science through Design-Based Learning versus Scripted Inquiry: Better Overall Science Concept Learning and Equity Gap Reduction." *Journal of Engineering Education 97*, no. 1 (2008): 71–85.

Muller, Karen, Erin Sharwell, and Stephanie Chase. "Meeting Patrons Where They Are: Experimenting with Shelf Arrangement, Community Service Points, and Non-Traditional Collections." *OLA Quarterly 21*, no. 2 (2015): 25–27.

Smith, Gudmund J. W, and Ingegerd Carlsson. "Creativity in Early and Middle School Years." *International Journal of Behavioral Development 6*, no. 2 (1983): 167–195.

4

A Makerspace Journey of the Middle and Elementary Kind

Jennifer Tazerouti

INSPIRATION AND RATIONALE FOR OPENING A MAKERSPACE

I was not convinced that my students needed a makerspace in our school library. We already offered lined paper, glue sticks, rulers, crayons, colored pencils and markers, a computer and a printer. Truly, what more did students need? My thoughts: makerspaces were just a fad that I was not ready to embrace, but attending a summer workshop about makerspaces changed my mind. I learned that a 3D printer was not a requirement; in fact, there really are no constraints. If that was the case, why was my collection of supplies not a makerspace? Looking back, I can say that those supplies allowed only flat, one-dimensional creations that were limited to book learning, poster making, and coloring. Makerspaces encourage building up, making models, 3D objects, and things that move. As Ana Canino-Fluit states, "Makers are people who make things rather than simply use them" (Canino-Fluit, 2014). The supply station in my library was meant to be consumed rather than to be transformed into something.

So why consider a makerspace? Libraries are an equalizing and empowering force in the world. Not all of our students have the benefit of the crafty parent or a garage full of supplies. The school library is the perfect location for a makerspace. It is staffed with people who supervise, consult, and collaborate. There are books and computers that students can use for information or inspiration on a project. Many school libraries have printers available, if needed, as well. The school librarian is familiar with the curriculum and the learning needs of the students. Having a makerspace in your school library can make it more of an equalizing force for the students you serve. The school library is the intersection of ideas and information. Making is a natural fit in school libraries (Craddock, 2015).

A few weeks after the summer maker workshop, while the students were away for the summer, I began to set up a makerspace in our middle school library, which serves students in grades six through eight. The makerspace was a hit, and I learned a great deal. At the end of that school year, I decided to take another position in a school that serves students from preschool to grade eight. My experience with the makerspace in my previous school was so positive that I immediately set up a makerspace in the library at my new school.

Adding a makerspace to the existing load of responsibilities may mean more work initially. What your school library's makerspace will look like and whether it is worth the extra time, effort, and money can be determined by analyzing what your school and community currently offers the students. If your school already has a makerspace, access to it may be limited. The makerspace may have a specific focus, such as engineering and technology. Outside of metropolitan areas, many students are not within walking distance to public libraries, museums, and other institutions that offer enrichment programming and resources. So the makerspace is their source of enrichment for them. Whatever form a makerspace takes, it has the power to broaden the range and scope of the library's impact on the students it serves. The materials and supplies found in makerspaces empower students to express learning in more creative and personalized ways. Here is how I created both of my makerspaces.

MY STEP-BY-STEP PROCESS

Supplies and Setup

The makerspace is really a combination of items, space, and the time to use these items and space collaboratively or independently. The supplies offered in the makerspace may differ from month to month or from year to year or be the same all the time.

Identify the Space to Be Used

In setting up both of the makerspaces, books had to be moved so that the shelves could be used for the supplies. I chose to interfile reference and our state book collection together. At the elementary school, I relocated our collection of upper elementary picture books and repurposed a book shelf that was previously used for book displays. In both spaces, I chose an area with tables and outlets nearby. Making can get noisy. Distance the area from quiet library areas when possible or designate a quiet reading area somewhere in the library.

Inform Stakeholders and Collect Supplies

In both instances, I decided over the summer that I would be opening a makerspace in our school library. I cleared the shelf spaces over the summer but did not do any more setup until after the school year began. At the beginning of the school year, I asked to be included on the back-to-school kickoff faculty meeting agenda to briefly tell teachers what a makerspace is and why I was planning to open one in our library. I told the faculty what types of items they could expect to find in the makerspace and also asked for donations of any items they thought we could use. I explained how, when, and why students would be allowed to use the makerspace.

Reaction of Faculty to the Makerspace Concept

At both the middle school and the K–8, there were some initial concerns about students being sent to the library for a particular reason and instead making something in the makerspace. It is important to teachers to know that their students are supervised when they leave their classrooms. I assured the teachers that we would do our best to see that students would be allowed to do only what was written on their hall pass to the library. Of course, it would be different if the student was visiting the library during nonclass times, which are before school, at recess, lunch periods, and after school. Even after my introduction and explanation, some teachers were skeptical, and some did not understand the need for a makerspace allowing students to use all of these materials outside of class. Some of these teachers simply needed time to see what happened with the makerspace. After seeing the space in action or seeing its impact on a child, most of the faculty was supportive of the makerspace.

Overall, the response from faculty members was very receptive after they had a chance to see the makerspace in action. Some teachers shared that they were often reluctant to assign take-home projects to their students since many of them did not have access to resources and supplies. One of the most encouraging comments that I received about the makerspace was that it would help students be able to create better projects. Another teacher told me that the makerspace helped her feel better about assigning projects. Most teachers are in favor of anything that will help their students.

Tell the Students about the Makerspace

At both schools, when students returned for the new year and came to the library for orientation, I told them about the makerspace. In both cases, they had plenty of questions for me. The first year I did this, I did not have ready answers for some of their questions. The students were very excited about this new addition to their library and asked questions like:

"You mean, we can come to the library and make whatever we want?"
"What if I don't finish what I am making?"

"Is there a limit on how many things we can make?"

"Does everything we make have to be for school?"

After seeing the students' enthusiasm, my answers changed. I was scared! The easiest question to answer was the one about unfinished projects. A space was designated for projects in the works. I told the students that we would talk about the details more the next time we met. Fielding these types of questions made me glad that I had not yet stocked the space with supplies. I felt as if I was flying by the seat of my pants, and it was a little unnerving. However, seeing the students' excitement was also exhilarating. This was obviously going to be a cultural shift for our students, and they would be getting new freedoms to test and explore.

STOCKING THE MAKERSPACE WITH SUPPLIES

After introducing the makerspace to the students, I sorted all supplies and put them in clear plastic shoe boxes. I labeled the boxes according to the contents. Sometimes a box contained only one item, such as cotton balls or yarn. Other times, multiple smaller items had to be combined in one bin, such as toothpicks and straws. I used large cardboard boxes and larger plastic tubs to hold the paper tubes, Kleenex boxes, recycled containers, and old toys.

In both schools, the principal included my request for donations—of old craft supplies, paper tubes, cereal boxes, tissue paper, beads, and the like—in the school newsletter. The response was overwhelming, and in both schools we received a considerable amount of materials. Requesting leftovers from craft projects or abandoned hobbies was effective, and we received donations from teachers and parents. We got yarn, stickers, old bulletin board sets, die-cut letters, glue sticks, tape, craft sticks, wrapping paper, felt, old toys, fabric, trim, and more. Some of the items were even brand-new.

I also spent some money on supplies for the makerspace. I purchased supplies from local big box stores and from a fantastic online source called NAEIR (National Association for the Exchange of Industrial Resources). NAEIR gets its inventory from companies who donate their overstock. Teachers must apply before they can make purchases from NAEIR, but the savings are worth the minor hassle of the application. NAEIR's catalog contains an ever changing list of goods for your makerspace. I purchased dry erase markers and erasers, sticky notes, metallic paint pens, duct tape, correction tape, and bookmark cross-stitch kits from NAEIR. When ordering from NAEIR, you often get a large amount of the item you are ordering. Shipping can take a while, but the savings make it worth the wait. I spent about $150 and received two very large boxes of supplies. (More details on supplies are at the end of the chapter.)

OPENING THE MAKERSPACE TO STUDENTS AND HOLDING A GRAND OPENING EVENT

Once the makerspace was stocked, I waited one more week before I allowed students to begin using it. I held a "grand opening" in conjunction with one of the parent nights our school held. For the grand opening event, I had student volunteers present and set up some simple stations that used the makerspace items. Stations included duct tape bookmark making, manipulative toys like Legos®, and tech toys such as Ozobots and Spheros.

When the makerspace was first opened to students, it was very popular. Each morning before the day started, I sent out 30 library passes. Some students arrive at school up to 45 minutes before school started. Why not allow these students to use the library? Before the makerspace opened, students came to the library to use computers, play board games, check out books and magazines, do homework, and read. The morning I opened the makerspace to students, every student who came to the library was in the makerspace. I stood back and watched as they explored the space and looked in the supply bins. Some of the students lost interest and went on to other parts of the library. Others remained in the makerspace. Quite a few students were interested in the duct tape bin. Some used the duct tape to decorate their school binders and folders. A few other students grabbed recycled paper tubes and plastic containers and applied duct tape to them. Some left their freshly duct-taped creations behind. The craft sticks and the glue gun were very popular. Students enjoyed making little houses with them. As I watched all of this, I began to worry.

I discovered that I was reluctant to allow students to come into the library and make whatever they wanted—giving them unrestricted access and freedom. Coming from the standard position of lacking resources, I balked at the idea of students devouring all the resources I had collected for them. I began thinking about rules or guidelines. It seemed that the students were hungry for this type of opportunity, but they were not sure what to do with it. I wanted as many students as possible to be able to use the materials and supplies I had gathered. The last thing I wanted was for a few students to come in, mindlessly use up the supplies, and leave nothing for other students who might need those supplies for a school project.

From that mindset, I decided that the rule for making in the makerspace would be that students had to create only items that were school related or for an assignment. I created a sign-in sheet and told students that they would have to sign in to the makerspace each time they used it, even though they already had to sign in to the library when they came in. On the sign-in sheet was a place for their name, time, date, and what they were working on. I decided that each student would have the opportunity to make one item that was not school related.

The sign-in sheet and the rule for making only one non-school-related item lasted about a month before I abandoned it. Two things happened that led me to stop using the sign-in sheet and rules. One, I was tired of constantly nagging the students about what they were making and what it was for. This rule was not compatible with the spirit of what I was trying to facilitate. Also, the student excitement about the makerspace had calmed, possibly as a result of the rules. I had to come up with effective ways of rewarding mindful making. I would take pictures of interesting creations or projects and post them to our Facebook or put student-made items on display in the library or the school's display cases in the hallways.

It may be necessary to have limits in place when the makerspace is first opened. At the K–8 school, the introductory rule was that students had to tell me what they were going to make. I either approved it or gave them another suggestion. I often sent students to the computer to look for ideas or to find an image that showed me what they were trying to create. We adopted the "plan, do, review" process.

Looking back on those experiences, I see that students being able to freely choose from available items is a culture shift in a school setting. In many cases, especially at the elementary and middle levels, students are given specific directions on what they are to do and how they are to do it. If students are given supplies, they are told how to use them. Students have to become accustomed to this freedom and learn to use their time wisely, not be wasteful, clean up after themselves, and be considerate of others. Students have to see that supplies get used up and possibly not be replaced before they become more mindful of their use of them.

A SIGN MAKES IT COMPLETE

Both makerspaces were set up and in use long before I put up signage. I wanted to make sure the makerspace concept was going to work out before I invested in signs. A sign is necessary to answer the question, "What's going on here?" In the middle school, I put vinyl lettering on the wall that said, "Make and Create." In the K–8 school, the district installed a makerspace sign that matched the existing signage.

PROJECTS AND CREATIONS

Here are some of the most meaningful ways the makerspaces have been used:

A sixth-grade science teacher asked her students to create a simple Rube Goldberg machine and make a video recording of the machine in action. Most of the machines the students made were easily taken apart, so the supplies were available to be reused. Although it was an independent project, students helped each other with video recording and encouragement. Students made use of the toy cars, marbles, dominoes, paper tubes, balloons, and many other items.

Students Using the Makerspace to Create a Rube Goldberg Machine.

A music teacher gave an assignment of creating your own instrument. Students loved being able to use their school free time and the makerspace to complete this project. When students looked through the available materials and became frustrated after trying to create an instrument, I suggested that they look in some of the books we had in the makerspace. The book *Unbored*, by Elizabeth Foy Larsen and Joshua Glenn (Bloomsbury, 2012), was helpful to a few students, as were YouTube video searches.

A math teacher's scale model assignment led to students using the makerspace in a new way. The teacher took items from the makerspace to use in her classroom. Since the library was carpeted, the teacher opted to let her students paint their creations in her classroom.

In a language arts teacher's totem pole project, students had to create their own totem pole. Some students did part of their totem pole at home and brought it to the makerspace to finish or to add items. In one instance, a student completed the majority of his project at home, but he did not have a screwdriver or a hammer and nails to attach the items to it. The makerspace tool kit saved the day.

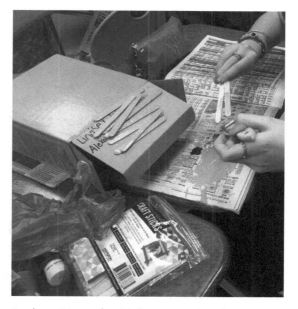

Students Using the Makerspace Supplies to Create a Scale Model Project.

I have held a few school-wide design challenges. Not all of them have been successful. My favorite design challenge was the cardboard gingerbread house project. A student who frequently visited the makerspace had the idea of creating gingerbread houses out of cardboard. The houses had to have a base, four walls, a door, windows, and a chimney. Students were not allowed to use any food items on their houses. Some students even tried to install LED lights in their houses. The houses had to be created at school. More students began projects than completed them. The prize was an actual gingerbread house kit. This was the first instance I discovered students hiding supplies to use at a later time.

A Hammer and Screwdriver Were All That Was Needed for This Student to Finish His Project.

One of Several Gingerbread Houses Created for a Design Competition.

A puppet show is one of those organic projects that prove the importance of makerspaces. It demonstrates the beauty of student-initiated projects that may begin with no curricular connections but that almost always end up with plenty of excellent curricular connections. In the K–8 school, a sixth-grade student was a frequent visitor to the makerspace. She was creating a puppet out of a recycled paper tube. Other students saw what she was making and joined her, each making his or her own puppet. Before long, the students had finished their puppets and began working on an antibullying puppet show. They utilized an iPad and green screen to record it. The students worked on their puppets and the puppet show for over five weeks. They collaborated, wrote, revised, and published their writing in the form of a recorded puppet show.

Students borrowing makerspace materials to work on projects at home is worthy of mentioning here. I created take-home bags after students came to the library to tell me they did not have the materials needed to complete the project and that they could not make it to the library during noninstructional times. In both cases, the students requested minimal supplies: duct tape, scissors, glue, and construction paper. I was happy to provide these items. Students brought the unused items back, the projects were completed,

Students Created Puppets and Used Them to Send an Antibullying Message in a Puppet Show.

and everyone was happy. I never had these kinds of requests before I opened a makerspace.

More about Supplies

Stocking supplies tip: Don't put everything you have out at once. Rotate items out and experiment with themes, if you have time. Students will have to learn to be good stewards of the supplies in the makerspace. My reaction to wasted materials is probably one of the biggest issues I have encountered. I want them to know that we are not dealing with an endless stream of supplies. Students who are conscientious makerspace users know they can ask me for certain items.

Here Is What You Will Find in Our Makerspace

(We rarely have all of these items in the makerspace at one time because we run out of them. Sometimes I do not have the funds to replace them.)

Staple items—Basic school/office supplies: regular paper, construction paper, glue, scissors, tape, rulers, poster board, markers, highlighters, colored pencils, chalk, pens and pencils, dry erase markers, boards and erasers, glitter, rubber bands, stapler, paper clips, recycled packaging such as egg cartons, plastic containers, paper tubes, newspapers, magazines, discarded books, cardboard, paperboard, tissue and cereal boxes, cookie tins, bubble wrap, packing peanuts, old CDs, stones, shells, discarded telephones, remotes, old board games, and puzzles.

If you do not have a makerspace, consider starting out with the following items to get your feet wet. Sometimes we have all of these things, sometimes we do not. Some of these items are stored "in the back" and only brought out are upon request.

Variable items—Yarn, string, ribbon, toothpicks, aluminum foil, wax paper, plastic wrap, straws, paper plates, plastic cups, coffee filters, marbles, dominoes, rubber bands, old toys, cookie sheets, copper tape, LED lights, coin cell batteries, beads, glue-on eyes, fabric, hot glue gun (only variable because we sometimes run out of glue sticks), brads, zip ties, popsicle craft sticks, magnets, Velcro®, cotton balls, pipe cleaners, cardboard cutting scissors, ink pad, stampers, cotton swabs, duct tape, hole punches, buttons.

The students really enjoyed the vinyl cutting machine that I donated and that also cuts construction paper and quickly learned how to use it to make monograms for their phones and lettering for projects.

Some of the items in the makerspace can become problematic. Rubber bands will usually have to be removed from the makerspace offerings periodically. One item that has been problematic is glitter. It just so happens that glitter is one of my favorite things. However, on a few occasions, students sprinkled it in one another's hair or threw it at one another. When items are abused in this manner, I remove them from the makerspace for a while and reintroduce them later. Another solution I have tried is to make the glitter available by request only. I have told students that they cannot have any glitter until their project is almost complete, and it has to be "worthy" of glitter.

The item that has the most impact in the makerspace is the glue gun. This is an item that students are often unaccustomed to using at school. I have a hot glue gun that I keep in the back and allow only certain students to use. The low-temp glue gun is always available as long as we have glue sticks. Most of the building projects completed in the makerspace depend on the use of the glue gun.

3D Printer, Vinyl and Paper Cutting Machine, Stop-Motion Station and Green Screen

Once I became more comfortable having a makerspace in the library and saw its impact on the students, I decided it was time to consider acquiring a 3D printer.

I applied for a grant and received a 3D printer for the middle school. I had no idea how to operate the machine or how to use the design software, but I knew the students would figure it out. When the printer arrived, I decided to let the students open the box and unpack it. Watching five sixth-grade boys unbox and set up the printer was probably one of the highlights of my entire year. From that moment on, the 3D printer became something that was theirs to use, theirs to show off, theirs to share, and theirs to "protect." The students taught themselves how to use the drafting program and then taught other students how to use it. We began printing already made items to see our 3D printer in action and then moved on to printing items we had designed ourselves. One student printed a premade dragon he downloaded from a library of 3-D printable objects. He took the head off, colored it, added a spring to it and made it into a bobble head dragon.

In addition to the supplies, vinyl cutter, and 3-D printer, I also had a stop motion animation station and a green screen area. The stop-motion/animation station is simply an iPad on a stand, with dry erase boards, markers, and erasers. Students can use Play-Doh or other items to create stop-motion animations using an iPad app. Our library already had three iPads before we opened the makerspace. Any of these can be used with the stop-motion station or the green screen. I purchased a heavy-duty iPad stand called a JustStand to be used in both of these areas. The JustStand enables the iPad camera to be used in several positions.

After Students Learned How to Print Ready-Made Objects, They Customized Them Using Makerspace Supplies.

CLOSING

Opening a makerspace to the students is interesting and challenging. The idea of opening a space in the library to create and tinker can be foreign and surprising to students. We as librarians want to see amazing things come out of our students in makerspaces. Sometimes the beauty of the makerspace is that it has that one thing the student needed to put the finishing touch on a project. The effect making has on students is a beautiful thing.

I had to learn to sit back and observe. Students putting duct tape around a paper towel tube and calling it a telescope may seem extravagant. Is it really? How can students benefit from this space and these activities? What are they doing that is beneficial? Often the process, or act, of creating is the Zen. I remember art class when I was in middle and high school. I did not like school, but I loved art class. I loved art class not because I was talented or skillful but because it felt good to use my hands to draw and paint and create. I also enjoyed being able to talk to my friends and being allowed to stand up while I worked.

Often a student will start a project and other students will see it and want to make the same thing. It is empowering for students to teach others how to make something. Impromptu opportunities such as this are what makerspaces are all about. A student can create a how-to video or offer a how-to session. These are important skills to nurture in our students. Learning and growth opportunities like this happen spontaneously sometimes. This is school at its best.

Some successes are organic. They just happen. You may not even know about them. How often are students truly given the freedom to create something that isn't graded, standards based, or related to an assignment?

Having a makerspace in my school library has shown me that people want innovation, change, or progress in small doses. Students want freedom in small doses. The school library is the perfect place for all of these things.

REFERENCES

Canino-Fluit, Ana. "School Library Makerspaces: Making It Up as I Go." *Teacher Librarian 41*, no. 5 (2014): 21–27.

Craddock, IdaMae. "Makerspaces @ Your Library." Workshop. South Carolina Association of School Librarians Summer Institute, Columbia, South Carolina, June, 2016.

5

The Makerspace Evolution

Sarah Justice

INTRODUCTION

Makeover, transformation, evolution—call it whatever you want, but in recent years a change has come to the school library. Libraries are usually dubbed the heart of the school. It is the one place where every subject and every curriculum converge and all students and teachers are welcome and invited. While some people stereotype the library as the dusty and quiet room that is used only for faculty meetings, others know the truth—especially the librarians. Librarians understand that the media center is ever evolving, and they see that this newest evolution of the makerspace is extremely beneficial to students and teachers. In the library, what once was thought of as the keeper of information has now become the cultivator of creativity. Libraries have always provided places for students to explore information, but, now with the inclusion of makerspaces, the library is providing students with the opportunity to explore science, art, and technology in a hands-on experience. As Josh Weisgrau says, "Libraries provide access [to] many print, visual, and virtual information resources that would not be accessible to most students and faculty, even in today's highly connected world. Makerspaces provide access to tools and materials that would be too expensive or impractical for most students or teachers to have as individuals or in a classroom" (Weisgrau, 2015, para. 4). For the past 17 years, the Rosman Middle and High School Media Center has provided students and teachers access to information and resources. During the past six years, it has also started to provide them with access to tools and materials not found in the classroom. The library has been transformed into a makerspace.

THE LITTLE LIBRARY THAT EVOLVED

Rosman Middle and High School is located in the rural mountains of western North Carolina. Until 2000, the school was grades 7–12 under the name Rosman Middle/High. After a school bond referendum in 1998, construction began on new additions that would allow the addition of a sixth grade and officially create two separate schools with two administrations. The Rosman Middle and High School Media Center was part of the new addition. In 2000, Rosman opened the school year with a total enrollment of approximately 750 students and one brand-new school librarian—Sarah Justice.

The library was designed as a traditional library. Computers lined one cinderblock wall, and the circulation area was a large multipart desk that was situated at the entrance/exit of the library. A large section of low shelving divided the room into two classroom-type areas that were outfitted with rectangular heavy wooden tables with six wooden chairs at each. All of the collection was located at the far end of the room on five tall shelving units and along the side and back walls. In all senses of design, it was a traditional library, but after getting a few years under my belt, it started to transform.

Gone were the bare white walls and the low divided shelf for reference books only. Gone was the massive circulation desk that guarded the entrance and exit. Gone was the alarm system that enclosed the doorway (it didn't work half the time anyway). Half of the heavy square tables were removed as well. Instead, round tables for collaboration and multiple workspaces greeted the students. Comfy chairs and area rugs designated reading and relaxation spaces.

The circulation desk was chopped in half and moved toward the center of the library so that students had easier access to help. The walls were painted in five different vibrant colors and student artwork adorned the wall. Classes came and went with regularity, book circulation was healthy, and all was good . . . until 2010.

In February of 2010, Rosman High School became the first 1:1 school in Transylvania County. As a 1:1 school, each of the students received an HP Netbook that they would use in class and be able to take home. Going 1:1 was great. Teachers became more innovative and started to incorporate more technology and more online resources. The students had the world at their fingertips. Unfortunately, the library suddenly became what every librarian fears—obsolete. At least it became obsolete in the eyes of the teachers. During those first few months, the only reason students and teachers ventured to the library was to get help with a technology issue. I became the go-to person for replacing

New Library Layout for a New Library Space.

keyboards (a task I never imagined I could do), reimaging computers when a virus popped up, and helping students find lost work on the network. I was no longer the go-to person for research help, book recommendations, or technology integration. What the library once provided—the only place to access computers besides the lab—now became part of the regular classroom. In the fall of 2010, the technology department hired an instructional technology facilitator, and suddenly even the reason students were coming to see me was filled by someone else. I became lonely and lost.

MAKERSPACE BEGINNINGS

I first started hearing about makerspaces at the North Carolina School Library Media Association annual conference in 2012. Librarians were starting to introduce arts and crafts areas, cardboard challenges, STEM items, and even 3D printers. When I first heard this, I thought to myself, "Hey, this sounds like something both my students and I would like." And it would help me get back to being the place and person that provided the "stuff" not found in the classrooms. So I started evolving. In *Learning in the Making: A Comparative Case Study of Three Makerspaces*, Sheridan and colleagues define the concept of makerspaces as being "comprised of participants of different ages and levels of experience who work with varied media, but a commonality is that these spaces all involve making" (Sheridan et al., 2014, p. 507). I have students that range from grade 6 to grade 12—a seriously large range of ages and experiences. I wanted to include items that all my students could use, and I wanted to appeal to all different interests. First, I wrote a Donors Choose grant. At that time, Donors Choose had a deal where if you had the first $200 donated, the MakerBot printer would be fully funded. I did not make that deadline, but I did get my project out there and I used the power of persuasion, social media, and even guilt to get the project funded. Some of the local residents were so intrigued by the idea that they donated without even really understanding what a 3D printer was. One graduate who works as an engineer donated so that students from a small, rural school would be exposed to technology that was usually reserved for larger schools or even colleges. I even stooped so low as to guilt people into donating the $5 they usually spent on their morning coffee at Starbucks. All of these tactics combined to successfully fund the project, ensuring that one major addition to the makerspace was on its way.

Before the addition of the 3D printer, the makerspace at Rosman Middle and High started with art supplies. Students were always in need of construction paper, cardboard, colored pencils, pens, scissors, and hot glue. I had hoarded these supplies for years. I am a huge fan of bulletin boards, so I had every color and texture of paper, along with shape cutters and fabric. Creating an art station was one of the easiest and most needed things I could do. Students now had immediate access to all the supplies they needed either for a class or just to be creative.

My hoarding skills came into play many times during this evolution, and I have found that I have become an even worse hoarder after seeing the success of the makerspace. Every item I see, I wonder how I can use it. The only way to reach the dumpsters at school is through the library, and my custodians have been known to stop by to ask if I am interested in something that is destined for the dump.

A sewing machine that was discarded from the apparel class had been collecting dust in my closet at home, so it quickly became a new addition to the library. Students used it to fix broken backpacks and to sew tears in fabric. After a rash of students crashing computer screens when they closed their Netbooks on their earbuds, we decided on a sewing lesson to avoid further damage. Using a pattern found on Pinterest, extra machines borrowed from the high school apparel class, and some fun fabric, we solved the problem. Approximately 60 middle schoolers became the proud owners of handmade earbud pouches. That left around 200 very jealous middle schoolers and a whole high school of students wanting pouches. Over the course of the next few weeks, students made pouches during lunch and any extra time in the day.

One of the greatest and most used additions to the makerspace was a manual typewriter. The students are fascinated, mesmerized, and completely perplexed by it. "How does this work?" "What does this do?" "Can I touch it?" "Oh my gosh, this is so cool!" These are all exclamations I hear on a weekly basis when students discover the typewriter. I have tried to establish a creative atmosphere surrounding the typewriter so that students can let their creativity take over. The device is set up on a small wooden desk covered by a lace tablecloth. A small flower in a glass vase sits next to it. A large metal shelf covered in magnets with poetry snippets printed on them is propped near it. The typewriter is just begging for students to write the Great American Novel. But usually I just find papers with random letters and a few odd sentences. Last semester, my student assistants began a typewriter war by composing pages of long letters to one another. Watching them painstakingly type out each message was hilarious. Recently, I added a second typewriter that was donated from a junk sale. Inside the carrying case was a note that read "To RJ From CJ, Christmas 1954." For history's sake, I kept the note attached.

A room switch in my own household led to the addition of a Lego® table. My sons no longer played with their train table, which coincidently had been a student's graduation project that I had purchased after completion, and I realized it would make a perfect Lego table. I later included a Lego wall that my construction class built. The high school students congregate around the table during lunch and build radical vehicles and outrageous houses. The middle school students are more creative and build animals, more cars, and even whole scenes. During after-school hours, the table and wall are favorites for the younger children of faculty and staff members.

Another addition was Snap Circuits. After my own children received a set for Christmas and I saw how durable, affordable, simple, but also creative they were, I knew they would make a great addition to the makerspace. Middle school and high school students all enjoy building with Snap Circuits. Many follow the directions and create the noisemaker or helicopter, while others just snap until something creates a circuit. Circuits are a newer part of North Carolina's seventh-grade science curriculum, so the addition of multiple kits to the library has helped the seventh-grade science teacher meet new standards.

The high school physical science class also visits the library during their circuit lesson and completes a lab using the Snap Circuits.

All of these simple additions to the library have helped to revitalize the space. The daily concept of the makerspace in the Rosman library is what I call a drive-by makerspace. Students wander in to check out books, pick up papers from the printer, or run errands for teachers, and they stop by the stations and build, create, or just play for a few minutes. They latch on a few Lego pieces, color a little on the coloring sheet, add some puzzle pieces, build a circuit, or play with the kinetic sand before moving on to their original task. However, given the time restrictions and the fact that some teachers were still not comfortable with a bit of chaos in the library, it was not an organized makerspace. To keep the students and teachers coming, I had to do more.

SUCCESS

So what has been successful for me? *Event days.* I started event days before I even created an organized makerspace. Each year that the elementary schools bragged about their Dr. Seuss's birthday celebrations, I became more and more jealous. Why couldn't we celebrate? Just because we are a middle and high school does not mean we cannot appreciate a great story. In 2009, we held our first Read Across America Dr. Seuss Day in the library. As with all my event days, I sent out an invitation to the teachers and did not have a set schedule. If they wanted to bring their class, they could. If they wanted to ignore the invitation, they could do that also. The day would last as long as my supplies held out. For our first Dr. Seuss Day, students could create Dr. Seuss hats out of cardstock and construction paper, *Daisy-Head Maisy* headbands, Grinch face masks, and Horton ears. They could egg-and-spoon race through the library shelves, play Dr. Seuss trivia, play Foot Book Twister, or watch Dr. Seuss cartoons. Stations for each activity were set up around the library, and instructions for each were posted with the supplies. In the beginning of the day, teachers were a bit reluctant to bring their students, but by the end of the day, students were begging to come, and the library was soon overflowing. And what probably also helped lead to that was the addition of a large cake and some "green eggs and ham" cookies from the local bakery.

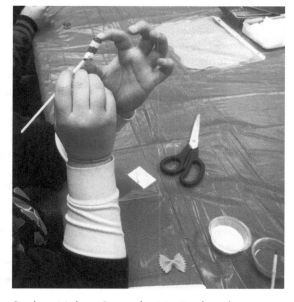

Student Makes *Cat in the Hat* Bookmarks.

Banner for International Dot Day.

In subsequent years, Pinterest has helped me to offer so much more to our celebration day. Students made *Cat in the Hat* bookmarks out of Popsicle® sticks and noodles, as well as Thing 1 and Thing 2 bookmarks using cutouts and blue yarn.

In 2014, photo booths were all the rage, so, of course, we had to have one for Dr. Seuss day. Students used cardboard props for mustaches, hair, and hats, and they posed with stuffed animals and Truffula trees. Hundreds of photos were taken that day. I also added a Dr. Seuss activity game that resulted in students running and jumping all through the library as they collected clovers using a Horton trunk attached to their head. It was quite a humorous addition.

Dot Day was added to my event day repertoire in 2014. Once again, this event is based on a children's book, but, once again, why does that mean that it won't work for a middle and high school? International Dot Day is based on Peter Reynold's book *The Dot* (Candlewick, 2003) about a little girl who realizes that she can make her mark on the world. It is a great lesson for us to teach all of our students, and it works well in a maker day celebration. Collaboration was an important theme in our Dot Day celebration. Students were encouraged to contribute to the "collabrodot," a long piece of paper to which each student added her or his own dot to, and at the end of the day, the art students used their skills to tie it all together.

This banner has been on display in the hallway all year long. Students also used coffee filters and washable markers to create drawings that they then spritzed with water to create amazing stained glass–looking artwork. Using the ColAR Augmented Reality app, we also incorporated technology into this maker day. Students used the Dot Day coloring sheet and created floating artwork. Students were so excited about this new app that many of them added it to their own phones.

The theme of 2014's Teen Tech Week was "DIY @ your library." This theme was a perfect fit for our makerspace and the recent addition of the 3D printer. Instead of doing one event day, I had a full week of activities. I was able to show off, in a fun way, the new tools that had been added to the library. Stations were set up for the 3D printer, Lego stop-motion moviemaking, bookmarks made from student photos, rubber band Wonder Looms, Washi Tape decorating, and

Lego building. During the week, students dropped in or were brought in by their teachers. During this time, it was also a great introduction to a lot of the teachers who did not realize what the library now had to offer. This week led to many new collaborations with different teachers.

One of the new collaborations was with the math teachers in the high school. These teachers always bring their classes to the library for event days, but we have not found common ground for collaboration until one teacher e-mailed me to ask whether I would consider a Pi Day event for the epic Pi Day of 3-14-15. Of course, I said yes. Pi Day included pi bracelets made using beads that matched assigned colors to numbers, trivia using a wheel of pi, number decorating that resulted in creating a library-length pi banner, pi tattoos, Twister (because it has circles, and I include Twister in every event day), and pi-themed foods like moon pies and pineapple orange juice. This year's Pi Day also included the game *Pie in the Face*.

Another collaboration that was a full maker day activity was in the collaboration with the sponsors of our Operation Christmas Child Shoebox group. Students in three teachers' classes created toys and games to be included in the Samaritan's Purse Operation Christmas Child Shoebox boxes. Stations included clothespin airplanes, tic-tac-toe boards, wooden spoon dolls, fabric pouches, shoe box top mazes, and Popsicle stick puzzles. Students made these items and then helped pack the shoeboxes for delivery. Students in the club also traveled to the local shipping area and helped pack and ship other shoeboxes.

The two most successful and exciting event days were based on Suzanne Collins' *Hunger Games* series. Many of the outdoor scenes of the first movie in the series were filmed in our county, and a few of our students and their relatives were extras on the film. With these connections, we had to celebrate the release of the film. The week before the film was released, we had an event day. Students played a cornucopia survival game, used makeup to create camouflage, learned to tie multiple types of knots, had a QR code scavenger hunt, and played *Hunger Games* novel trivia. We also had a costume contest in which a surprisingly large number of students and teachers participated. Because of the success of the *Hunger Games* event, it

Wooden Spoon Doll.

became expected that I would have a *Catching Fire* event and make it even bigger and better.

Since this event had to be epic, I called in reinforcements. Our occupation course of study English teacher had read *Catching Fire* with her students, and we had worked on curriculum connections with her students by creating stations that the students rotated through. The students asked whether they could create a Hob area (the black market in the novel) and run it during the event day. Each shop would have items for sale, and students could purchase these items by bringing in canned goods. Those canned goods would be donated to the local food pantry that the students worked in for service hours. The students did all the preliminary advertising, created the signs for the booths, priced all the items, and were in charge of the station until all the items sold out. After the event, we donated over 500 items to the food pantry.

During the original *Hunger Games* event, one of the stations was for camouflage, where students could use makeup and nail polish to create their Capitol look. This led to quite a bit of spilled polish, ground-in makeup, and a significant amount of ruined carpet. The custodians were not very pleased with me. Since *Catching Fire* has even more scenes that deal with the Capitol's excesses and style craziness, I had the brilliant idea that I needed a professional on hand to do makeup and nails, but I had no money for that, and I really did not think that anyone would volunteer. After some brainstorming, I realized that our local community college offered a cosmetology and esthetics program, so I called the director to see if someone could help. And help they did. The class was actually held that day in my library. The students brought their kits and let their artistic skills fly while their professor advised and taught them proper techniques. My students had their eyes made up, faces painted, nails painted, hair colored, and tattoos added. The lines for each of the 15 cosmetology students were six deep at a time—an excellent example of community collaboration.

In the maker areas, students created duct tape roses in President Snow's rose garden, made bow and arrows from Q-tips and dental floss at Everdeen's Archery, and dressed in wigs and costumes for the photo booth. I borrowed the Katniss and Peeta standees from the local Subway restaurant so students and teachers could have their pictures taken with the victors. It was a nonstop, highly successful event day. At one point, every single class from the high school was in the library participating. Even though we have had multiple event days since then, nothing can live up to our *Catching Fire* day.

NEXT STEPS

Event days are still worked into my schedule each semester, and we have celebrated Dot Day, held Pi Day, and created Christmas toys, but lately I have been moving toward lessons in the library using the "stuff" I have that classrooms do not. Snap Circuits have brought classes to the library for labs, and so has the Hot Wheels set. In 2016 and 2017, I received a grant to rent a *National Geographic* Giant Traveling Map. For two weeks, I taught lessons on a 25×35-foot giant map of Europe (2016).

We measured traveling distances from one city to the next, identified different land formations, and even followed the path of World War II during our visit to Europe. In 2017, we traveled the solar system with the giant map. Forty-four classes visited the library during the eight days of the map. Each discipline at the school could participate and fulfill objectives in the North Carolina curriculum. We also held a STEM night for parents and community members.

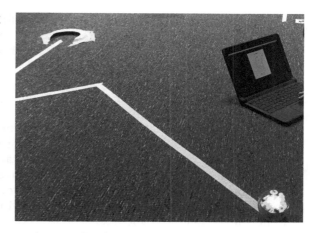

Students and Spheros.

After attending a workshop in November 2016 that included using Spheros in the classroom, I purchased a lab pack of 12 of these small, easy to code, robotic balls. I already owned two, and the only activity I had figured out to do with them was chariot racing with world history classes. While this was a lot of fun for the students, I really did not feel that I needed to purchase any more Spheros. But after attending that workshop, I immediately bought them. During Hour of Code week, the library was transformed into a putt-putt course. Students used their Chromebooks and the Lightning Lab app to program the balls to travel the course.

Physics students conducted a velocity lab using the Spheros, and physical science students programmed them to do a long jump into pans of sand. They altered the angle of the ramp to try to achieve maximum jumping distance. After studying Jackson Pollock, an art class created paintings in his style using the Spheros. The collaboration with these teachers has been wonderful because they are experts in their subject areas while I'm the expert in this technology use. It is a perfect partnership. After the students were introduced to the Spheros during class, many of them began using them during lunch in the library. They have become experts on driving, racing, and programming these tools.

My most recent integration is a Google Expedition kit. During the solar system map visit, I was able to use devices and Google Cardboard collected by our county technology department. After the success of this, I pooled some finances and ordered a kit for my library. I hope to be drawing in more classes with the virtual reality experiences very soon. As new technologies and new ideas come around, I know I will keep adding and changing.

WHAT TO KEEP AND WHAT TO ABANDON

So you want to try your hand at this? My advice is to do what works for you and your students. I have tried many things and abandoned many things. I am glad we have a 3D printer, but it does not fit into my program very well. I do not have the time with the students to teach them how to design, and I do not even have the higher-level programs for them to use for designing. Students do use free online programs such as Tinkercad to create, and I am more than happy to print things the students design, but I am no help to them with the design itself. So do not think that you have to have a 3D printer to have a makerspace.

Always remember, making is messy. Even though I am a cluttered person with a desk that is piled high and an office that has stuff stuck everywhere, I know where everything is. There are spills, stains, and many unidentifiable messes that no one tells you about. Students use materials in ways you never intended, and they can be wasteful. All that comes with the territory. You have to come to terms with it and realize that something great is happening.

I know it is cliché, but you also have to step out of your comfort zone. In the past two to three years, I have been teaching about topics that I have no background in and at times no clue as to what I am even talking about. When I was teaching about Europe on the Traveling Map, I learned so much just by the questions of my students. I had to find answers to those questions. When I was in school, there were nine planets. On the solar system map, there were eight. I really had to brush up on my solar system knowledge. Physics? I was lucky to pass chemistry in high school, and that is the last time I saw a science class as a student. But you better believe that when I was working with the Spheros and the physics class, I did my best to appear to know what I was talking about. I am at least comfortable pleading ignorance and then finding the answer with the students. So get outside of that box and start being a bit uncomfortable.

Finally, find teachers that will work with you, and then the others will see the awesomeness and follow. I have a great relationship with my high school art teacher, and I love the projects we do together. She is willing to do anything, and I am happy to brainstorm with her. Steampunk art has become my favorite lesson, and the results are great additions to the library displays. It was an experiment when we used the Spheros for Jackson Pollock–style art. The art teacher had

Students Create Pollock-Style Art Using Paint and Spheros.

never seen a Sphero, much less thought about using it for artwork. But between the two of us, we made the connection that made for an amazing maker activity. After that class, one of the students said, "This is so much more fun than real classwork!"

THE BEST WORST THING

My many years in the library have been filled with amazing learning experiences. In the past four years, I have changed more than ever. Going 1:1 with laptops felt like the worst thing that could happen to me; I felt as though I was becoming obsolete. But after some self-reflection and program reflection, I realized that this worst thing was actually the best thing that could have happened. It made me refocus and recreate my space. I advocate for my library all the time and find that social media is the best way to show the world what is happening within my four walls. I am at the point in my career where I am teaching the children of former students. After seeing some of our activities online, one of those former students questioned why she did not get to do the fun stuff like her daughter does in my library. She was jealous. I love where my library has been and where it is heading. Creating a maker culture and an exploration space keeps every day exciting. As Mr. Lemoncello explained, I am creating a space where students can learn "how extraordinarily useful, helpful, and funful—a word I recently invented—a library can be. This is their chance to discover that a library is more than a collection of dusty old books. It is a place to learn, explore, and grow!" (Grabenstein, 2013, p. 75).

REFERENCES

Grabenstein, Chris. *Escape from Mr. Lemoncello's Library*. New York: Random House, 2013.

Sheridan, Kimberly, Erica Rosenfeld Halverson, Breanne Litts, Lisa Brahms, Lynette Jacobs-Priebe, and Trevor Owens. "Learning in the Making: A Comparative Case Study of Three Makerspaces." *Harvard Educational Review 84*, no. 4 (2014): 505–531.

Weisgrau, Josh. "School Libraries and Makerspaces: Can They Coexist?" Blog. Edutopia. September 24, 2015. https://www.edutopia.org/blog/school-libraries-makerspaces-coexist-josh-weisgrau

Part III

Upper Grades

6

Student-Led Makerspaces

Phil Goerner

INTRODUCTION

Our library is really amazing. Located on the Front Range in Longmont, Colorado, Silver Creek High School educates approximately 1,300 students. The library serves as a teaching and resource center, providing information resources and collaboration with staff and students. It has been designated as a Highly Effective Library through the Colorado Department of Education, which means our library has been recognized not only for our leadership, 21st-Century skills, and our collaborative work with teachers but also for the positive impact we have had on student growth and achievement. The library is truly the hub of the school, hosting and instructing many classes a day, as well as meeting the needs of walk-in students intent on increasing their academic achievement and pursuing individual interests.

The real meat of what we do is to collaborate and team-teach with classroom teachers in every subject from physical education to science, from English to integrated studies. We teach the library science skills, and the teachers fold in the subject matter. We are also a 1:1 iPad school where each of our students and teachers is given a device, so the library serves as a 21st-Century skills learning hub where we not only fix glitchy problems but also share cool apps and best practices for utilizing technology for teaching and learning. Our active library also hosts numerous clubs and activities, such as Anime Club, book clubs, Forensic Club, leadership activities, author visits, and even a lively and competitive poetry slam every month.

Despite the depth of our services, our students wanted more, they needed more. Silver Creek has a leadership focus, which educates and encourages its students to develop leading roles and collaborative relationships with the community, as well as management skills, self-direction, and innovative, independent thinking. The school began offering basic introductory programming classes, so many of our students were already exploring these skills. They have the aptitude to become engineers. They are experimenting with drones, app development, diagramming electrical circuits, and even designing and creating their own skis. As a library team, we thought we were ready to introduce a makerspace, and even though we were not sure how it would look, who would use it, where it would be housed or what would be in it, we had a pretty good idea that the students would be ready for it.

BUILDING THE MAKERSPACE SUCCESS

In order to be successful, we made several visits to Tinkermill, our local adult makerspace. This was a terrific way to see some really good ideas, the layout as it worked for them, and some very fancy as well as very simple tools. They were generous with their time and open to chatting with us and sharing some very good ideas. In fact, our initial outreach allowed us to form a relationship with one of their organizing board members, Dixon Dick, who took us up on the invitation to volunteer in our space once it was set up. He has turned out to be one of the most valuable assets to our entire makerspace.

What we learned in real life from Tinkermill was supported by makerspace articles like "The Philosophy of Educational Makerspaces" by Kurti, Kurti, and Fleming, which stated, "Effectively run makerspaces can invite curiosity, inspire wonder, encourage playfulness, and celebrate unique solutions while ensuring that it is okay to fail and that breaking things is not a cardinal sin. The creation of a safe space for exploration also encourages students to collaborate, collaborate, collaborate" (Kurti et al., 2014, pp. 10–11).

Dixon and I found these goals to be essential, foundational factors we wished to incorporate into what we were creating. We also did lots of research of maker librarian blog sites and posts, who posted about their space and what items were being purchased for their students, the many different ways librarians were setting things up, what was working for them, and even where they submitted requests for funding. Since there were no makerspaces in my district to visit, we spent time traveling to STEM schools and vibrant libraries in adjacent districts to learn about their resources and how their leadership was shaping their schools.

From these experiences and research, we developed lists of tools, resources, and ideas in order to write an initial grant with DonorsChoose. As we looked for a location, we knew we had to respect the many students coming into the library as walk-ins seeking the quiet study spaces the library has always offered. However, there was a room off the library that had been many things since the school opened and most recently was a computer lab. The computers had been recently removed, so we commandeered the space. The takeover had begun.

JUST A START—FUNDING AND UNPACKING

Our grant was filled in a short period of time. We were excited to purchase some basic supplies in our original grant request from DonorsChoose: "Help

Bring Backbone to Our Makerspace." We also had submitted a second set of grants that allowed us to purchase the building's first 3D printer.

When the items arrived, we made a *big* deal of it with our students, and we promoted and planned an Unpacking Party where students could join us in unpacking and assembling everything. You would have thought it was a festive holiday! The students poked and prodded, sniffed, and ogled! They unpacked and set things up. The students who attended the unpacking party became our core makerspace group, and they quickly decided to meet weekly to explore each one of the Makerspace resources in depth.

The first students explored and learned about the Sphero rolling robot balls. The kids quickly got the hang of it and formed teams to level up their Sphero, winding it through pylons and going over the jumps. Before they knew it, they were learning some programing and operating skills while expertly guiding their mini-robots around the library. Of course, there were Sphero races in the main school hallway and invitations for our principals to join in the fun! The students became quite knowledgeable quickly and were excited to share what they had learned with new stu-

A Student Operates the Sphero.

dents. This student sharing, teaching, and learning together are what became the backbone of our makerspace.

The students had an awesome time the week we explored our Cubelets®, which are magnetic blocks that can be snapped together to respond to light, sound, and temperature to do simple tasks. The students were so engaged and in the questioning mode that the time just flew by. "What does this do? How

Students Working with the MOSS Robots.

does this change that? What would happen if we . . . ?" Who knew six little Cubelets could be so versatile and remarkable? The Modular Robotics company has since added MOSS robots to the mix, which are incredibly versatile robot construction kits that our kids use to create extraordinary inventions from land rovers to fork lift–like transports.

We also explored the circuit board building and experimenting kit, known as Arduino, and Snap Circuits, which are electronic circuits that students can snap together. Our students were quickly snapping and clipping electrical circuits together, knowing that time was limited, but they were eager to learn all they could! More and more questions helped to propel students and adult mentors alike to the point where all were anticipating their time in the makerspace, thinking about and regarding what they had as something useful, interesting, and amazing.

Students were so proud of what they learned that they decided to hold an open house on parent–teacher conference night to share what they had created. Students designed fliers to advertise the event and sent invitations. On the evening of parent–teacher conferences, each student operated a station where they expertly explained and answered questions about their particular makerspace resource while sharing the excitement and passion about the possibilities that each resource held. It was a well attended, fun, and amazing night.

A Student Creates a Snap Circuit Masterpiece.

One of the strongest aspects of our school makerspace was the early partnership we forged with Dixon, the board member from the adult makerspace Tinkermill. When he asked whether he could be involved during the student gathering times, I realized he really knew his stuff. He approached me as an engineering consultant and business entrepreneur saying, "I know engineering, software, and how to organize and plan for success, but I don't know kids and you do. You teach me how to relate to kids, and I'll be happy to share what I know with them."

As we chatted, we realized we wanted to incorporate a combination of project-based learning strategies, as well as peer-to-peer interactions. We knew that if we designed our makerspace right, we could use project-based learning strategies, such as posing open-ended prompts or essential questions, in a way that would initiate, engage, guide, and encourage our students to expand their own learning (Waters, 2014). We wanted these questions to propel students' desire to learn more and perhaps help them begin the process of designing their own learning. But as Walters says, "Making requires partners," so we focused on developing an environment where collaboration was essential. Working on projects they were passionate about and mentoring one another side by side would "increase student engagement while empowering students" (Walters, 2014, para. 5, 2014).

Eric Mazur (2011), in his studies of peer instruction dating back to 1991and 1997, demonstrated how collaboration strengthens learning and that students can often figure things out more easily if they share their learning with others. Consequently, we thought it would be more impactful if students, rather than the adult mentors, shared what they had learned with other students about components of the makerspace. Just as Mazur's research had discovered, our students were very excited to share what they had learned with one another. Since the students had only recently learned the skills, they still knew what the difficulties were and how to break the learning down for their peers.

ORIGIN OF THE BOX PROJECT—PEER INSTRUCTION

Together, Dixon and I developed a process of student-to-student shared learning we called the BOX Project. We talked about how one student would teach the basic attributes, safety, care, operation, and nuances of an individual makerspace resource to another student, who would then demonstrate his or her mastery of the skills by creating project. Since we were printing a series of boxes on the 3D printer as we were talking, we decided to call this the BOX project.

The challenge to students was to use the BOX metaphor to demonstrate their mastery of a makerspace resource. The process would basically follow these steps. A student who wanted to use a resource must first find another student to mentor and instruct that student on how to use it and create something based on the BOX metaphor. Then, we would take pictures of these successful students with their BOX projects and add them to a poster so that other students who wanted to learn how to use a specific resource would know who had already mastered the resource. Students could also receive a 3D printed badge celebrating their mastery if they wished. Once students held their BOX Project achievement on any resource, they were free not only to mentor and instruct other students about that resource but also to investigate or create more complex projects exploring additional attributes of that resource.

A Student Programming Lego Mindstorms.

So what does a BOX Project look like? On the 3D printer, it is somewhat easy to imagine. Students can select an object that looks like a box as a model for their first build. They would then learn how to change filament, level the table, adjust the settings, sand/paint or finish their print, as well as anticipate and avoid challenges that might keep their project from being successful.

What does a BOX Project look like on something else like a Sphero, Cubelets, Snap Circuits, 3D pen, or even the green screen? What we have found is that kids are incredibly creative in designing their BOX Projects. Kids learn how to program the Sphero to go in a square (or box-like) formation. For the green screen, one student danced in a box while another climbed into a cardboard box, which then flew away into space. A student created a tetrahedron, a 3D triangular box, to demonstrate mastery of the 3D pen. Using Lego® Mindstorms®, another student created a forklift that picked up a box. No two BOX Projects are alike. They reflect individual student interests. For the BOX Project challenge, students encourage and mentor one another, asking and answering questions while learning together.

Of course, some students experience frustration and difficulty learning a new resource. What we have found is that student mentors help to channel that frustration, encouraging students to persevere. It is so gratifying to watch students struggle and eventually overcome hurdles! Students, with specific outcomes in mind, are determined to learn what they need in order to achieve success. Students ask what they want to know from a mentor student, and this often triggers additional curiosity, propelling more learning. Learning has become the student's responsibility and joy! They are so excited to try something new, even if it does not work, that their brains are fully engaged with the neurons firing. "Curiosity is triggered, and students can't wait to become experts in answering their own questions" (Wolpert-Gawron, 2016, para. 4).

In the makerspace, students ask nonstop questions, and they are eager, even impatient, to find answers. The students are *so* curious about everything! Research tells us that we are on the right track in that the questioning propels the learning. "When curiosity had been piqued by the right question it puts the brain in a state that allows it to learn and retain lots of different kinds of information. The students are jazzed about their learning and can't stop sharing what they know" (Stenger, 2014, para. 5).

Questions drive even more questions in the makerspace, but they were never more apparent than when the students were exploring the Makey Makeys. Our students are natural gamers, but when they found out that they could use a banana for button pushing to play a vintage game, they were ecstatic—"What else will conduct?" No available fruit in the building was safe! These teens explored every available object, including one another. What could be more fun than walking in and seeing seven teenagers holding hands to make a button beep?

Once students complete their first BOX Project, they explore their first resource in greater depth, or they move on to create BOX Projects of every other available resource. Regardless of the resource they are using, students are able to build on what they have learned to create something new. The completion of that first project is a building block, igniting further exploration and learning.

GROWING AND EXPANDING

Magazines and Web sites have been very inspiring in helping students create something new. One of our students saw a Skycam in *Make* magazine that incorporated a 3D printed base for a programmed Raspberry Pi and camera. He was hoping that, when the project was completed, it could slide on cables to terrorize students in (and out) of my library. The student was *so* ready to start making this project. He began printing the frame, ordering the necessary parts, and programming the Raspberry Pi.

While we loved his enthusiasm for the project, this student taught us the importance of making a build list and teaching project management skills. Many of our students seem to be weak in visualizing all the steps necessary to lead a project to fruition. Taking the time to carefully research all the parts needed for a build, as well as budgeting the time needed for completing each step, is something we've learned must be modeled and taught. Since our students meet only at lunchtimes and after school once a week, they need help setting small, short-term goals so that they can successfully complete larger projects.

We have exceptional students as well. I nickname everyone, so a brilliant freshman I call New Girl had an idea to create something new. She is one of our makerspace students, but she is also participating in a special 20% time project in her art classroom. Her innovative art teacher is encouraging the students in her classroom to choose to combine the subject of art with some other passion. New Girl has exceptional interests. Not only has she learned about Raspberry Pi's, 3D pens, wood burning, circuits, and soldering during the normal makerspace hours, but every other Friday she spends her normally scheduled art class time in the makerspace as well. The idea she pitched to her art teacher was to create a robot to hold a special drawing tool combined with a spinning canvas.

Her unique art project involves programing Lego Mindstorms, crafting tools to hold a brush or pencil, and coordinating the motors to spin the canvas. She has been working independently, reporting to her art teacher after every session with blog posts and pictures. She is developing into an organized, motivated student who loves to learn and is not afraid to make mistakes.

We have found that another driving incentive for our students is to create something that helps others. An example of this happened during the second year of makerspace when we found that one of our middle schools in the district was also creating a makerspace and trying to start by building a Lego wall. They had no money and very few resources once the Lego wall was installed. Once our students found out about this, they organized a Lego drive and were able to collect box after box of Legos to send to the middle school.

In another instance, a few of our members went on a field trip to a STEM middle school with me to learn about their Engineering Brightness project. The notion of the program is to design and solder LED circuit boards combined with a battery pack placed in a specially designed 3D printed lantern case. After the lanterns were built and tested, the goal was to send them to a group of students in a third world country that was experiencing rolling electrical outages. The students could then Skype with the students who received the lanterns, learning about one another's classrooms while talking about the design of the lantern. My kids soldered, wired, and designed on the field trip and brought all their ideas home. Now deemed the Circuit Girls, they have redesigned the lantern and are just about ready to send their own lanterns to a faraway classroom. There is something about a philanthropic project that seems to give incentive to my students

PRESENTATIONS AND COLLABORATION

To return to New Girl and her makerspace/art project, things have not always gone smoothly. Often when perplexed, New Girl will explain her project to another student in order to think aloud. While explaining her project, other students will ask for clarification, and this process helps New Girl refine her thought process and design. Through this collaboration, New Girl often solves problems and finds interesting next steps to try to move her project forward.

This interaction is something we try to encourage in each of our student's work. When students complete a portion, a project, or even have a big success or failure, we really want our learners to formally share their learning. There is great value in hearing about the independent projects that others are doing, so students are encouraged to make either formal or informal presentation to other students about their process and project.

This type of communication and collaboration helps not only the student presenting but the other students in the makerspace as well. Student projects are often quite awesome. Sometimes projects are incomplete or nothing works, but we celebrate the learning that these failures bring too.

Not only does this help others who are trying to do similar things, but it also helps students analyze how they approached their projects. We also find that when students present about something they care about, they really just focus on telling the story. This has the added benefit of helping students improve their communication skills and confidence, at the same time usually gaining positive feedback.

Given enough support and resources, our students create their own learning too. One day when I was late, the students were already gathered around the projector for a class by the time I walked in. One of the makerspace students was in the process of instruction on how to design a 3D object using the free online tool, Tinkercad. He was soliciting

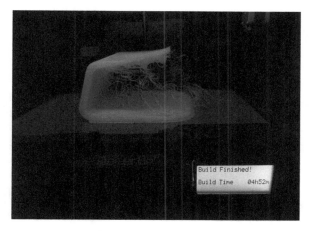

Epic Design Failure on MakerBot 3D Printer.

help from his peers in printing and designing the 3D printed base for the Engineering Brightness project. So, quite indifferent to my presence, students conducted their own exploration and ended up staying an hour and half after school to learn something new. Amazing.

Since they are excited about their work, they often collaborate well. One example of this is a student who was building a chariot using the SAM Lab Bluetooth® motors, switches, and tools. He was creating a mashup using Lego Mindstorms with SAM Lab. It is actually quite remarkable. He set up a simulation where he has a slider switch for each motor attached to a chariot harness, and he views and programs the variables through the Bluetooth connection on his laptop.

He ran into a glitch where the axles on the motors he was using were not the right size, and they would not fit snugly in the connection. Another student heard about his issues and began working with him to design an axle that would work

A Student Proudly Displays His SAM Lab Lego Mindstorms Magnificent Mashup.

A Student Creates Time-Lapse Videos.

using the free online Tinkercad software. After several tries, both students have now designed and tested a workable solution. Each student used personal skills and strengths and collaborated to create something new.

Another example early in our makerspace history came when my students were working with the incredibly slow laptop we had inherited to collaborate with our 3D printer. "Mr. G, your laptop is *awful!*" was a constant complaint. Therefore, I asked the question I always ask: "What are you going to do about it?" In a short brainstorming session, the students decided to raise the money and then build their own machine. This was a great opportunity for students to write fund-raising letters, which was a challenge but fruitful. One English teacher who helped the students edit and refine their letters said that the lead student was more focused and working harder on this project than he had for most of the semester. One student even began visiting funding boards. After one such visit, he told me, "I wore a suit and a tie because we are asking for a lot of money."

After several weeks and many, many visits, the students ended up getting plenty of money pledged to gather the parts to build a raging fast and robust computer. With the help of our advisor, the final build pieces were ordered, and the construction party was scheduled. With all available makerspace students present, the build was completed with a time-lapse video to prove it! The wonderful machine was built and is a testament to student willpower.

These stories show that when our students are passionate and motivated, they are driven in their learning in ways that we cannot always predict. They are persistent and resilient and quickly learn that not everything always works out well the first time, but through grit and determination, they can find success. If they have the tools and can collaborate with others, they can create amazing things.

RECOMMENDATIONS FOR THE FUTURE

When we acquire a new resource for the makerspace, my partner Dixon always reminds me to "give it to the students. Tell them a little bit about it, and they will figure it out. Just watch." They do create. They do build. In addition, most importantly, they do ask questions because they are the ones who have to figure it out.

We will keep writing grants, sharing our stories with administrators, and recruiting teachers and members of the community. We will collect partners and projects to build. We will make things and wreck things, all the while developing relationships with the students and the students with one another. We will keep encouraging our students to become talented people who stick with stuff.

We really feel it is important to grow and change. We are also preparing for a very crowded future in our building. One way to share the joy is to take the makerspaces into the classrooms. To this end, we have been looking at some type of mobile lab or cart contraption to show off our services and gadgets. Who knows what this might look like! It would be good to explore this in order to integrate into classrooms better. Can you imagine social studies or language arts with a green screen or math class printing 3D circuits or volume measures? We also think our kids are ready for field trips to local technology sources and learning hubs. We are lucky because locally we have SparkFun™, Sphero, and even Google only a bus ride away!

RECOMMENDATIONS FOR OTHERS

If you are thinking about adding a makerspace to your library or classroom, consider your goals. From our experience, the more student centered, inquiry based, peer instructed, and project based you can get, the stronger the learning will be for the students. The students are the ones who are telling us which tools they need, what questions they have, which drones they want to fly, and which gizmos they want to build. It is up to us to figure out how we are going to help them.

I would suggest you contact someone you know who could help you. Build a team with a teacher, a librarian, and an administrator. Not only do our students need to collaborate, but it is essential that we work with other geniuses as well. We all do something well. I challenge you to share what you are doing with someone else. Post your work, your students' successes, and your hard-to-fix moments. We are all better when you do. Be open to new learning and sharing because when you do, you are bound to experience something incredible.

Do not wait until you have enough tools, the right resources, the perfect space, or the right students and teachers. You know what your environment is and what your students need. Start with that. You will be amazed with what your students will teach you. As my educational partner Dixon always says, "Give the kids the problem. They have the tools to figure it out."

REFERENCES

Kurti, R. Steven, Debby L. Kurti, and Laura Fleming. "The Philosophy of Educational Makerspaces Part 1 of Making an Educational Makerspace." *Teacher Librarian 41*, no. 5 (2014): 8–11.

Mazur, Eric. "Rethinking the Way College Students Learn." 2011. http://americanradioworks.publicradio.org/features/tomorrows-college/lectures/

Stenger, Marianne. "Why Curiosity Enhances Learning." December 17, 2014. https://www.edutopia.org/blog/why-curiosity-enhances-learning-marianne -stenger

Waters, Patrick. "Project-Based Learning through a Maker's Lens." July 9, 2014. https://www.edutopia.org/blog/pbl-through-a-makers-lens-patrick-waters

Wolpert-Gawron, Heather. "What the Heck Is Inquiry-Based Learning?" August 11, 2016. https://www.edutopia.org/blog/what-heck-inquiry-based-learning -heather-wolpert-gawron

7

The Inclusive Makerspace: Working with English Language Learners and Special Education Students

Gina Seymour

OUR JOURNEY

It's hard to say when Islip High School Library's makerspace actually began. In reality, we've encouraged a maker mindset for many years. From cooperative puzzle making to the time students built a 5-foot High Holiday tree made from reference books, we're a school library that embraces collaborative making. Noisy, messy, hands-on library programs and events have been routine for years. Celebrations such as Teen Tech Week and Computer Science in Education Week are celebrated annually. However, it was about four years ago we decided to set aside an area to create a dedicated makerspace area in our school library. Over the course of time, the physical space and the program have expanded greatly in response to participation. Islip's makerspace program began with simple supplies such as puzzles, recyclables, and several donated K'NEX engineering and construction building sets. A few tech-based kits focusing on creating electrical circuits, such as Makey Makeys, littleBits, and Snap Circuits, rounded out our initial selections.

In our open access model, students could visit the library during lunch period and use the makerspace. Initially, with our limited resources, smaller groups such as English language learners and special education students were the first to participate as whole classes. At the same time, individuals could always come in and tinker on their own, without a classroom teacher, making use of this open model, a practice that continues to this day. Not having a class set of 30 items allowed me to work with special population students on a regular basis. As more funds became available, the resources increased, as did the collaboration with general education classes. Now the makerspace is used daily by varying classes and individual students alike.

THE THREE Es OF SCHOOL MAKERSPACES: EQUITY, EDUCATION, AND EXCITEMENT

The act of making and tinkering helps our students develop critical thinking skills and creative problem solving in an environment that encourages collaboration and communication (Fleming, 2015). Making promotes *equity*, *education*, and *excitement* for all students but in particular for our special needs populations such as English language learners (ELLs) and special education (SPED) students. School library makerspaces are inclusive learning spaces making a variety of materials and supplies, as well as academic content, available to all students.

Equity

Makerspaces provide accessibility to resources that students may not have available at home due to financial circumstances and, as such, supports equity among all students. Expensive coding robots, iPads, and other costly supplies are not financially accessible to all students. Robots such as Dot & Dash and littleBits circuits can be a costly investment for any family. Even a relatively cheaper option, the small codable robot Ozobot, at $50, is still out of reach for many students. However, this needn't restrict their exposure to these resources. Through resource sharing in school library makerspaces, all students can access materials to enhance academic and personal learning.

Education

Due to an unforgiving academic load in learning English, ELLs are deprived exposure to activities and course content in a traditional learning environment. The situation is similar for special education students. SPED students require additional academic intervention support time in content area curriculum, reducing their access to electives. In the dynamic setting of a school library makerspace, these students can explore a range of topics from computer science to physics through classic makerspace activities such as Hour of Code and building circuits. Code.org offers coding in over 30 languages, allowing inclusive participation regardless of language proficiency. Similarly, robots need not speak only English but can be programmed to speak any language desired. Time available in the schedule for course electives, such as sewing classes, is rare for most of our special needs students. However, these students can still learn to sew using our makerspace sewing machines. This accessibility to supplies and educational learning concepts, leveling the playing field for all students, has been referred to as democratized learning (Fleming & Krakower, 2016).

Excitement

While cleaning up an afterschool maker session, a teacher of English as a new language (ENL) and I discovered writing on one of the newspapers we put down to protect our tables from hot glue gun usage. "I ♥ school" was written. We were not sure who wrote the message as we had ELLs, SPED students, and general education students working together on a community project. Though it really doesn't matter who left the message, what matters most is that the teens had a positive experience. How often do you hear high school students exclaim that they love school? While in our makerspace, students are generally happy and smiling because they experience success within it, and they like that feeling. It is hard to sit all day and listen to lectures, fill in worksheets, or take tests only to receive marginally passing grades. The experience becomes demoralizing and drains self-esteem. As part of an assignment, one of our ELLs wrote me a thank-you note for hosting a maker activity with his class. In it he said the activity "was fun because it make [sic] us break the routine, also I enjoy making and crafts." Kinesthetic activities challenge and engage students by providing intrinsic motivation.

Learning Strategies

Multimodal learning strategies for working with ELLs and SPED students include employing visual, auditory, and kinesthetic activities. In our makerspace, we always use the recommended strategy of providing visual cues in our instructions (Fleming & Krakower, 2016). Many of our monthly independent challenges are set up on a table with supplies and instructions, ready to engage individual students during their free periods such as lunchtime. Having instructions with visual cues assists our independent learners and our visual learners, and it benefits students with limited reading proficiency. Many maker sets are color based such as Snap Circuits and littleBits. Each color corresponds to an action, making the instruction manual easy to follow with limited reading ability or language proficiency. To promote English language acquisition, effective classrooms exhibit several characteristics, many of which are inherent to makerspaces. For example, classes should be meaningful, authentic, and interactive with enjoyable activities; include relevant topics, be engaging, and include interactive small groups (Dormer, 2016). Hands-on, project-based activities are highly beneficial in fostering learning by doing and offer students a break from the routine of sitting and listening all day.

OUR STORY: THE INCLUSIVE MAKERSPACE

The acquisition of knowledge through imaginative thinking and hands-on discovery is a key part of Islip's program. Our open access model encourages student visits during lunch periods and unscheduled periods. Students can work individually or in self-selected groups. Many of our special needs students start off using the makerspace on their own by themselves, but over time become very comfortable interacting with others in the space due to increased self-confidence. Makerspaces invite collaboration and communication, and for ELLs and special education students this is a key benefit. "What is that?" or "What are you doing?" is frequently heard as classmates observe makers. Curiosity is leveraged to increase learning and conversational communication skills. Often ELLs and special education students are uncomfortable speaking up in a formal academic environment such as in a classroom. However, when showing off a new creation or cool robot, they take on new personas. Poised, self-confident, beaming with increased self-esteem, these students can succeed and thrive. Using newly acquired confidence, they communicate and teach others using both academic and conversational vocabulary.

We started off with low-tech projects using recyclables when working with general education classes of 25 or more students: birdseed ornaments for the ornithology class and balloon-powered cars for science- and physics-related content. The necessary materials were inexpensive and plentiful. We initially handled offering more costly tech projects by requiring sign-up and promoting these activities during events such as Teen Tech Week, as funding was not available for multiple whole-class sets. Also, as with any new programming, there were uncertainty and wariness regarding participation. As word grew of the dynamic and engaging learning opportunities, so did participation on all levels, from students to teachers. Initially, we always had supplies for smaller groups, so working with teachers of special needs classes worked out perfectly, albeit unintendedly.

Using any item in the makerspace to build and explore, some students tinker for just 40 minutes while others work on projects requiring days or weeks to complete. Our makerspace is large enough to adequately maintain numerous works in progress. We work with class sizes ranging from five students to 30. Routinely working with ELL and SPED classes allowed the students to become acclimated and accustomed to being in the library. Even though we hosted fun, engaging activities, programs, and events, prior to habitual collaborations with special needs teaching staff, these students didn't participate much, particularly our English language learners with limited language proficiency. This is no longer the case. Our students are so comfortable and accustomed to visiting the library that they now independently visit during lunchtime and after school. Indeed, students from both subpopulations now frequent the library regularly and sign up for special events as well.

Some of our special education staff use the makerspace as a reward. If the class stays on task and completes the week's assignment in the classroom, then they may use the remaining class time to visit the makerspace. This puts in place intrinsic motivation. These visits are of the nature of a drop-in model, and tinkering is on the menu as opposed to a structured class project activity.

Students are highly motivated as they relish the opportunity to choose their own activities rather than following directions, which they get enough of within the classroom setting. Special education staff may schedule group class activities in the makerspace in advance. Through collaboration, librarian and teacher can discuss student and curriculum needs, as well as review student individual education programs (IEPs).

INDIVIDUAL EDUCATION PROGRAM (IEP)

Students receiving special education services require individual plans designed to meet their needs. These documents are referred to as individual education programs (IEPs). We currently have several special education students whose IEP goals reflect time in the makerspace. As indicated on one student's transitional assessment, "[H]e likes to fix things and . . . he would like to use his technology skills to help people solve problems." Transitional goals assess a student's strengths, preferences, and interests. Transition-related goals can include "occupational awareness, effective personal interaction, and the development of potential career goals" (O'Connor, 2009, p. 14). Using the makerspace can help students meet their individual IEP goals, such as breaking down tasks, managing time, correcting for outcomes, and decision making. Developing social skills, such as interacting with others, is another typical IEP goal. Small collaborative groups thrive in a makerspace environment. In my experience, shy, nonverbal students, over time, consistently grow into self-confident, boisterous teens when engaged in building, tinkering, and making.

Directions utilizing visual cues provide an additional skill of following directions, as one would need to do on a standardized test. Practicing this skill in a fun, nonstressful manner, even when mistakes are made, show that the failure can be fun. Failure, such as a balloon-powered car that runs in reverse or an LED circuit that won't light up, is the best part of learning in a makerspace. Besides a few good laughs, students learn an engineer's mindset: They learn to keep tinkering with and tweaking the project through analysis and observation until they are successful. For educators, if grading is a must, then grade the process—not the product. Students can succeed through successful failures in that learning takes place and the student uses critical thinking skills to attempt problem solving. Assess the determination, grit, critical thinking, and problem solving that took place as opposed to the aesthetic end product. For ELLs, determine how much collaboration and communication occurred while attempting to solve a problem. Use of conversational, as well as academic, vocabulary in this setting should be encouraged and rewarded.

LANGUAGE ACQUISITION IN THE SCHOOL LIBRARY MAKERSPACE

Verbal positive reinforcement by the teacher-librarian is valuable, though not as much as the positive reinforcement received through successful encounters in the makerspace. Using language skills to accomplish a self-motivating task in a makerspace is "a new way of engaging in English" (Maio, 2016).

Students want to tinker, create, and make, and to do so, communication needs to take place. The makerspace is ideal for the acquisition of conversational and academic vocabulary. Successful language learners are willing to take risks and are willing to make mistakes, and educators need to encourage risk taking (Dormer, 2016). A major factor in language acquisition is self-confidence, and positive reinforcement enables ELLs to gain confidence. Makerspace activities are perfect for encouraging risk taking as many students feel as though they are playing. There's no number two pencil in their hand and no stressful assessment before them. Our teachers of English as a new language use a room in the library for testing, which is to the right. Our makerspace is located to the left. Students are all smiles when veering to the left, and frowns abound when they are redirected to the right. The makerspace is self-motivating, and our ELLs have become so comfortable in our makerspace that they come on their own without teachers or advisors, regardless of their language proficiency. They recognize that they will be successful and feel safe within our space. This is an added bonus.

MAKERCARE: SERVICE PROJECTS

In 2016, we added a dedicated community service model to our maker area that we call MakerCare. This section of the makerspace promotes civic engagement and social action as students work on community service projects to donate to various agencies. Often themselves the recipients of services, ELLs and special education students can switch roles by giving instead of receiving. Community service is a typical requirement of our honor society students. Community service participation among special education students leads to a strong sense of accomplishment and self-esteem. Our English language learners frequently volunteer in our MakerCare center, giving back to the community through service projects. As an added benefit, they learn about agencies and organizations in their new community by participating in making items to be donated to those agencies. Service can make English language learners feel more connected and accepted at school and within the community, while reinforcing language skills through authentic engagement (Russell, 2007).

A popular activity this year was the making of cat and dog toys that were donated to our town animal shelter.

Many ELL students did not know that we had this agency and that it was located within

Easy to Make Upcycled Dog Toys.

walking distance of our school. Another successful project was the I Found a Quilted Heart activity in celebration of Random Acts of Kindness Week. This activity was open to all; however, several teachers of English as a new language signed up their classes for participation. We sewed decorative fabric hearts that were then left in random places around school or town for others to find. After a vocabulary lesson on the meaning of the word *random*—there was some confusion—students got busy making their hearts. The teacher and I were privileged to overhear a conversation in which one student questioned, "Why do we need to be nice to strangers?" Her classmate responded, "So we can make new friends." Then a third student chimed in and related the conversation to what they had been discussing in the previous class regarding bullying: "There will be less bullying if we're nice to one another. We need to be nice to others so they will be nice to us." Bullying can be a concern for special education students and ELLs alike. We hadn't planned on discussing bullying and kindness, it just occurred. Makerspaces promote conversation and communication, and you never know where the conversation will lead. I have learned so much about my students (one girl visits her grandmother, a seamstress, in Poland during the summers). No wonder the student was so adept at sewing these fabric hearts. In the relaxed atmosphere of making, an educator can get to know students and their stories as positive relationships form. Students begin to feel more comfortable in the library, in the makerspace, and in seeking me out in the hallways when they need assistance. Through this supportive endeavor, the social emotional needs of the student are met. Service "does more than help students learn and improve academically; it also teaches them to reach out to others, to take pride in and ownership of their community, and to learn and improve as human beings" (Russell, 2007, p. 771).

WE NEED DIVERSE MAKERSPACES

If there's one thing I've learned since opening our makerspace, it's that change is inevitable. The ability to remain adaptable, open, and flexible almost seems to be a prerequisite. So it is no doubt that we will continue to expand our programming. In what direction that expansion will go remains to be seen, although moving forward I would like to see an increased emphasis on empathy. *Merriam-Webster* defines *empathy* as "being aware of and sharing another person's feelings, experiences, and emotions" (*Merriam-Webster*, 2017). Developing an empathetic mindset benefits society because empathy is one of the stages in the design mindset. In order to engineer and design an item, the maker needs to understand its use and the end user. Seen as a critical and an early step to design making, "[E]mpathy is always where the solution begins" regardless of the problem or challenge (Egbert, 2016, p. 30). Diversity in the makerspace allows students to engage in new experiences and understandings. We need diverse makerspaces.

Inclusiveness and diversity benefit not only the special needs student but also the general education population through positive experiences with differently abled peers. Diversity in the makerspace provides meaningful connections to peers by learning about one another in a unique, fun, productive way.

A mix of students with cultural differences, mixed physical abilities, and differing languages and learning abilities adds to the dynamics of your makerspace. Can a wheelchair fit in your makerspace? Do you have visual images next to word labels on your storage boxes so that all students can find supplies independently? Do you have left-handed scissors? Right-handed students are baffled when witnessing a left-hander use a regular pair of scissors. This exposure to a range of differences and increased awareness permit understanding and empathy to develop. From there, new design thinking can occur. We are not only educating students academically but also preparing them to become the next generation of design engineers and creative problem solvers.

We like to mix ELL and non-ELL peers to increase conversational communication skills and to build meaningful connections and experiences among peers. Increased awareness and acceptance of students unlike themselves, whether culturally or physically, enhances diversity in the makerspace.

RECOMMENDATIONS

You are the connector between educators at your school and your maker program. Speak at faculty meetings, send e-mails, or just approach any willing faculty member to discuss what you have available to offer. Initially, staff members will be confused and not understand what the makerspace has to offer. Others might mistakenly assume that maker activities are for and geared to talented and gifted or for honors students as an enrichment program. Many on staff might not be familiar with the maker movement. With all this in mind, be proactive and offer professional development training workshops, and speak at department meetings for special education staff and for teachers of English as a new language. Be sure to invite all staff to participate in any maker events or challenges you host. Even if just one or two faculty members show up and participate, you'll have free word-of-mouth advertising among colleagues. Often, staff members approach me because their students, either verbally or physically, shared their lunchtime maker activities. The curious teachers then make their way up to library to investigate; this is your opportunity to open up a dialogue and collaborate. Reach out to special education staff and teachers of English language learners. Support faculty by facilitating lessons and by providing ideas and supplies. Ask which units teachers are working on or are upcoming, and then think about ways you can provide relevantly themed, curriculum-based activities. Remember, working together, utilizing each other's professional strengths, benefits all students.

Collaborate to include special populations so that all students can take advantage of the resources and activities offered in your makerspace. Exposure to cross-curricular content using hands-on learning strategies empowers special needs populations through increased self-esteem and confidence. Don't hold back on activities or refrain from presenting your students with a wide range of skills and experiences. The diverse makeup of your student body adds to the dynamic experience. Language and learning ability are not barriers because making transcends both. School library makerspaces facilitate student-centered learning where the needs of all learners can be met. The key point to remember is that making is for everyone.

REFERENCES

Dormer, Jan Edwards. *What School Leaders Need to Know about English Learners.* Alexandria, VA: TESOL Press, 2016.

Egbert, Megan. *Creating Makers: How to Start a Learning Revolution at Your Library.* Santa Barbara, CA: Libraries Unlimited, an imprint of ABC-CLIO, 2016

Fleming, Laura. *Worlds of Making: Best Practices for Establishing a Makerspace for your School.* Thousand Oaks, CA: Corwin, a SAGE Company, 2015.

Fleming, Laura, and Billy Krakower. "Makerspaces and Equal Access to Learning." July 19, 2016. https://www.edutopia.org/blog/makerspaces-equal-access-to-learning-laura-fleming-billy-krakower

Maio, Pat. "'Makerspaces' for Science Instruction Also Proving Helpful for English Learners." November 30, 2016. https://edsource.org/2016/makerspaces-for-science-instruction-also-proving-helpful-for-english-learners/572782

Merriam-Webster. "Empathy." April 17, 2017. http://www.wordcentral.com/cgi-bin/student?book=Student&va=empathy

O'Connor, Michael P. "Service Works! Promoting Transition Success for Students with Disabilities through Participation in Service Learning." *Teaching Exceptional Children 41*, no. 6 (2009): 12–17.

Russell, Natalie M. "Teaching More Than English: Connecting ESL Students to Their Community through Service Learning." *Phi Delta Kappan 88*, no. 10 (2007): 770–771.

8

Stepping Back: Letting Students Lead the Makerspace

Lucas Maxwell

INTRODUCTION

Glenthorne High School, in South London, is a mixed academy for ages 11–19 that specializes in the arts. Considered "Outstanding" by the UK's OFSTED (Office for Standards in Education), it is a very popular and successful school dating back to its opening in 1958.

I started working at the Glenthorne High School Library in 2013. Previous to this, I had spent close to five years working with teens in a public library in Canada. The Glenthorne Library was opened in 1999 by popular UK author Jacqueline Wilson. It had two floors; the downstairs housed all of our nonfiction and fiction and had enough tables and chairs to accommodate around 40 students. The upstairs had 30 computers and a bookshop where we sold school supplies. The library's makerspace would start in this library but wouldn't really take off until we moved into our new library.

The library moved into its new location in May 2016. In comparison to its previous location, the new library is more than triple the size and can hold over 1,000 more books, bringing the total number to just over 6,000. This was a much needed change, considering the school has over 1,500 students. It is now located in the heart of the school and is one of the first areas that greets you as you enter the building. It has 30 PCs and a large television screen for students to use before school, during break and lunchtime, and after school.

Glenthorne's First Open Mic.

We offer a wide range of before- and after-school activities, like our Manga and Film Club that attracts a diverse group of users. On average, the library circulates more than 1,000 books and is used over 15,000 times every month.

LITERATURE REVIEW

The first time I became aware of the maker movement was from watching Mark Frauenfelder from Boing Boing and *Make* magazine being interviewed on the Colbert Report. *Make* is bimonthly and focuses on DIY projects of all kinds, from more advanced robotics to simpler woodworking projects.

From listening to Boing Boing's Gweek podcast, I learned about a book called *Unbored: The Essential Field Guide to Serious Fun* by Joshua Glenn and Elizabeth Foy Larsen. The book is chock-full of games, fun survival tips for children, crafts activities, and a lot more. It really is essential if you want to ensure that you get away from the television for a few hours and have some fun doing really engaging and positive activities. In fact, there's a whole line of these books now that contain a ton of great information ranging from games to hiking and adventures. The best part about them is that they put you, the reader, in charge of your own fun and teach you how to do it in an interesting and enjoyable way.

I would be remiss if I didn't mention the book *Invent to Learn* by Sylvia Martinez and Gary Stager. It discusses the very beginning of classroom makerspace ideas to tips on incorporating makerspaces into several aspects of your school life.

After following people like Colleen Graves, Tiffany Whitehead, Diana Rendina, Nikki D. Robertson, and Jennifer Lagarde on Twitter, I became more aware of the impact that makerspaces could have on both the student body and staff at a school level. Through them, I became aware of littleBits, a circuitry set that makes learning fun and essentially error free. It is very hard to make a mistake with littleBits. Sure, you can set things up wrong, but you quickly learn how to navigate through the components. It makes learning fun and simple. I was instantly hooked and purchased my littleBits Base Kit right away for Glenthorne.

MAKERSPACE JOURNEY

Creating a makerspace was something that I have wanted to do since I began working as a teen librarian in the public library field in Canada. I had watched a demonstration of a 3D printer at one of our sister branches and was instantly hooked. Although I did not end up having a 3D printer at the branch I worked at, the makerspace bug was in me, and I was determined to start one in whatever capacity I could.

In Canada, it started with zine making. Zines were very popular in the late 1970s during the short but powerful punk rock movement. Whether you believe that punk rock began in the UK with the Sex Pistols or that the Sex Pistols took their ideas from grimy bands like The Stooges and the Ramones is up to you. The zine movement was a way for people interested in alternative music and culture to stay on top of where their favorite bands and artists were performing. In the case of the Sex Pistols, police would often shut their shows down in advance, so they had to rely heavily on guerrilla marketing and promotion in order to avoid mainstream attention (Blandy, 2003).

I wanted to create a punk rock type of movement in the library. No, I did not want teens to destroy the place. I wanted them to embrace the DIY movement and start creating their own zines. I was very fortunate to discover that zine making was alive and well near the public library that I worked at. Located within an old house on a quiet street in the city of Halifax is a print shop/zine-making den. Local artists will come in, along with bands and authors, to drink coffee, make T-shirts for their gigs, or simply hang out among the 5,000-plus zines they have on hand (Nauss, 2014).

I approached this group and offered to buy some of the zines they had. They refused to take my money and instead gave me a giant box of them to show to the teens that I worked with in the library. It was a great way to get started. I ran a series of zine-making workshops and even had some of the artists from the house in Halifax visit the library to deliver a few sessions on how to make your own zines. I also visited the local high school and started a zine club. We were the first public library in Nova Scotia to officially catalogue zines that students were making and allowing other people to borrow them. It was a great feeling to see them go off into the world; it made both the teens and me proud.

Because the library had never had a qualified librarian at its helm before I began, creating a makerspace had to be put on the backburner. It took a little while to get the collection organized and to assemble a team of Student Library Assistants, so I was not able to focus on creating a makerspace until my second year.

One of my first jobs was to get an army of students to assist me in getting the word out there that the library was about to make many changes. To do this, I started the Student Library Assistant program. In the first few months, I recruited five students that came in during break and lunch to assist with questions at the information desk, straighten shelves, borrow and return books, and assist with our Film Club. They chose the films, made posters and lunch passes, prepared the room to watch the film, and helped ensure everything was neat and tidy when the film was over. They also helped write some reviews of the films we watched and encouraged other students to take part. We were lucky enough to get Film Club ID badges from Into Film, an organization in the UK that provides schools with free films and film-related goodies to run film clubs. I soon recruited some older students to act as monitors as the library was on two floors and the Library Assistant and I were not always able to keep an eye on everything.

Student were interviewed prior to receiving their post as Student Library Assistants. I did this to create an atmosphere of professionalism and to let them know that I took their hiring seriously and that they should as well. This worked out very well in the end because it meant I was able to recruit students who were genuinely interested in the position. Out of the first ten that eventually became Student Library Assistants in 2013, four are still working in the library on a daily basis as Assistants, currently undergoing their fourth year in the library.

As a reward, the students receive Achievement Points every time they assist in the library. After a certain number of Achievement Points, they receive gift cards to local shops. I also provide them with lunch passes so they can jump the long lines that fill the hallways every day. At the end of each term, I hold a pizza party for them to show my gratitude. I am glad to see that the seeds sewn in 2013 have come to fruition because the four Assistants I mentioned earlier have become pivotal in starting the school makerspace and helping me deliver it to students.

OUR SCHOOL'S MAKERSPACE STORY

From the very beginning, I knew that I wanted students in charge of the makerspace. I wanted them to know that the library was *their* space and that I trusted them to lead a popular program. My opinion is that student learning is best when they are in the driver's seat. Yes, I am the backseat driver but a nonannoying one that gently helps steer them on their way. I had delivered a very successful run of open mic sessions once a month for a few years straight.

This program was led by older students who set up the equipment, made the set list, and recruited their friends to play. Aside from doing a quick introduction at the beginning, I left it up to the students to create an atmosphere where they were in charge of the event. The only rule was that there was to be no offensive lyrics, of course!

The next program that I started in 2013 was a manga club. Manga is a popular

Glenthorne's New Library, Opened May 2016.

comic book style that originated in Japan. The thing that stands out most about a manga comic is that you read it from right to left. Manga are commonly joined with an anime, or Japanese animated television show. Manga and anime's popularity was low when I was working in the public library in Canada, but when I moved to the UK I saw how huge it was.

When I began my position, the library had a half a shelf dedicated to 12 ratty copies of the "Death Note" manga. Now we have 12 shelves full of manga, and the collection continues to grow. In order to ensure I am buying manga that reflects the needs of the students and is age appropriate, I created a Padlet where students could let me know which manga the library should buy. Padlet is an online "wall" where you can collaborate with others. For example, I created a Padlet asking the students what manga the library should own and gave the students the password to my wall; they log in and anonymously write their responses. It can be difficult to purchase manga that is appropriate for young teens and even slightly older teens. I recommend viewing the article written by Brigid Alverson for the *School Library Journal* for a great guide on manga that is appropriate for your teens (Alverson, 2015).

I see the creation of the Student Library Assistant program, Manga Club, and the Open Mic as the true beginning to the makerspace. I had three great programs off the ground at an early stage, and I had a needling in the back of my mind, a desire to create a program where students taught other students valuable skills.

Once we moved into the new library space, I was more determined than ever to incorporate the makerspace into our existing programs. The place to start was our weekly Manga Club, which has had a dedicated following since it started over three years ago. In Manga Club, I began experimenting with basic crafts. We made origami eyes (Manga fans are obsessed with eyes), duct tape wallets with manga characters on them, manga bookmarks, and much more.

These were the most popular programs, and I soon had over 30 students wanting to take part. The challenge was that I did not always have a Student Library Assistant in the library after school, so I had to recruit the more mature members of the club to help. Eventually, this challenge went away because the program had attracted members from ages 11 to 16, so it was easy to nominate a few people to show the other students how to do the craft or take charge if something else demanded my attention after school.

At lunch, I ran a tutorial on making the bookmarks with our Student Library Assistants and had them deliver the program after school to the 20-plus other

Members of Glenthorne's Manga Club Making Duct Tape Bookmarks.

Mini Canvases Made by Glenthorne's Manga Club.

students who arrived for the event. I was on hand to ensure that everyone had enough material, but overall the Student Library Assistants led the program and that was the goal in the first place.

In addition, the Manga Club used 4×4-inch mini canvases and made their own manga masterpieces that they were able to take home. This required little setup or leadership because the students knew exactly what they were supposed to do once they were handed their canvases.

The students have also made page corner bookmarks, blackout poetry, and several other crafts. The Manga Club has been an effective arm of the library's primary makerspace. With the Manga Club a success, I decided to ask those students to properly promote our makerspace. The first thing I wanted to do was to brand it, make it something that would stand out and be consistent with every program that we ran.

As usual, I went to the students and the Library Assistant for guidance. I already knew about Kristina Holzweiss's SLIME (Students of Long Island Maker Expo) and I wanted to create something similar for our library that stood out. After lots of debate and acronyms, we finally settled on the SLAM Club—Student Leaders and Makers.

We put SLAM on all of our posters, we made bookmarks, and we promoted it on the display screens in the hallway and in group assemblies where we were able to speak to over 700 students on a weekly basis to promote our activities. I would not have been able to come up with the idea without the help of the Library Assistant or the Student Library Assistants.

To begin the SLAM Club, I purchased a Lego® set and several different kinds of duct tape

Comic Book Bookmark Making in the Library.

(if you do an Amazon search for duct tape, you will find that several different duct tape patterns are available). I also purchased K'NEX and books on Lego ideas and duct tape crafts. K'NEX are made up of wheels, cogs, and thin plastic tubes that interconnect. The response was overwhelming; students were lining up to interact with the stations that I made. Each station was on a separate set of tables, with a sign clearly labeling the station and the appropriate books on the tables. My plan during those early days was to set up the makerspace every Friday at lunchtime. This would change once we moved into the new library, but it was a great way to introduce the students to the makerspace.

Lego Station at Glenthorne's Makerspace.

Our major successes have come with the simpler makerspace programs: easy crafts, bookmark making using old comic books, keychains, and magnet and button crafts. The button maker has been by far our greatest success. I rented one to make Harry Potter and Roald Dahl buttons during World Book Day here in the UK; we made over 100 buttons in less than 30 minutes. This was again led by a Student Library Assistant; I gave her a 2-minute tutorial on how to use the button maker just before the program started and then let her host and deliver it. We had so many students wanting to make buttons that I had to extend the program to after school.

Again, once students found out that buttons were being made in the library, we were

Duct Tape Station at Glenthorne's Makerspace.

flooded with requests to make more, so I rented it again to help launch our first ever Comic Con, which we held on a Saturday in the school. We had several students come to make badges, comic book bookmarks, and eat loads of free doughnuts.

Another success has been with littleBits, which are electronic building blocks that use magnets to let you connect in order to invent a wide variety of home-made electronic items. I find littleBits very intuitive, and any fears that I had on how complicated students would think it was soon fell to the wayside. I let students play around with littleBits, and it was very rewarding to see them explore it and figure it out on their own. In the case of the three sessions I've done, I've given them instructions on how to do specific projects if they want, but I feel that they've had more fun messing around with it and creating their own circuits and inventions.

CHALLENGES

There are always challenges with starting a new library program. The first challenge is your own brain. You need to tell yourself that you will not lose your job and the school won't collapse if nobody shows up to your duct tape wallet-making program (speaking from personal experience). Once you overcome that fear, things will be a lot easier for you.

Another challenge is knowing your audience, especially your Student Library Assistants. Try to find things that you know they would be interested in as much as the students that are taking part in the program. This will generate excitement on everyone's part, and that kind of enthusiasm in infectious.

A challenge that I have consistently experienced is not anticipating how busy students currently are. I know that there might be several students who want to come to a lunchtime makerspace activity, but they already have several other commitments that prevent them from doing so. This is why I am consistent with the makerspace's time and place. Lunchtime on the third Friday of the month seems to have hit a chord with the students (for now), and I am happy to keep it that way. Running the makerspace too many times a month might be popular at first, but it would soon run out of steam in my opinion. Again, it is important to establish what your students want before going in at full speed. Having the makerspace once a month also means that the Student Library Assistants can prepare in time and deliver the program with some knowledge under their belts.

The big challenge that everyone will undoubtedly mention is money. I know how fortunate I am to have such a supportive Senior Leadership team that trusts my decisions to deliver programs to the students that will benefit them during their time at the school. That said, I know I am probably an exception to the rule and that a lot of librarians and educators out there think they need bazillions of dollars to start a makerspace. As I have already mentioned, you do not need that kind of cash. My advice would be to start small, and then see what works for you and what your library users are interested in doing. Once you have established their needs, then you can slowly move on to bigger and (hopefully) better things.

PLANS FOR THE FUTURE/CONCLUSION

My hope is that I can have a dedicated makerspace in the library. I currently have the material in boxes and out of sight. I would love to have an area clearly defined as the makerspace where students can enter and take part in hands-on passive maker programming. I also want to increase student involvement. I would like the Student Library Assistants to develop their own programs on a more regular basis. The challenge with this is that it eats into their rapidly diminishing free time and/or homework time.

Thinking back to my time as a teen librarian in the public library in Canada, watching that 3D printer demonstration still inspires me to try to have one for my own in the library. The challenge is space, money, and time to ensure that the students get the most use out of it.

I am a firm believer in bringing in guest speakers, no matter what the medium. I do tons of author visits, both in person and via Skype and Twitter chats with our student book club. Thinking along those lines, I am very interested in bringing in a series of "experts" to teach making to students. I am thinking about people in the construction industry or in science, wherever I can find them. Students respond to guest speakers; it is like a breath of fresh air when someone different comes into the room to speak. Bringing new faces and energy to the library's makerspace would really propel it along a path that creates a true feeling of community within the school and the surrounding neighborhood.

If you are interested in starting a makerspace, the biggest hurdle is often a fear of failing. My advice is to start small and to gather allies in the form of Student Library Assistants and other staff members interested in helping out. Throw some ideas out there, promote it to death, and be prepared. If you fail, try another makerspace activity. It will take a little while to figure out the right groove for your school and your students.

My next piece of advice is to get permission to create social media accounts for your department. Twitter has changed my professional life for the better, not just on the makerspace level but at all levels. Use social media to find out new ideas, gather feedback, and collaborate with like-minded professionals. You will find that they are more than happy to provide meaningful advice and give you free ideas to start your makerspace.

My makerspace journey has been one that is led primarily by the students. I did this by creating a strong Student Library Assistant program before doing anything else in the library. Again, this might not work for all libraries, but it has been very helpful for me in setting up, promoting, and delivering the makerspace to as many students as possible. I am constantly trying to evolve what a makerspace means within the library space, and I'm very excited that this transformation includes a strong student voice

REFERENCES

Alverson, Brigid. "15 New Manga Series to Freshen Up Teen Collections." School Library Connection. 2015. http://www.slj.com/2015/07/collection-development/15-new-manga-series-to-freshen-up-teen-collections/#_

Blandy, Doug. "A Brief History of Zines." Duke University Libraries. 2003. http://
library.duke.edu/rubenstein/findingdb/zines/timeline

Glenn, Joshua, and Elizabeth Foy Larsen. *Unbored: The Essential Field Guide to
Serious Fun.* London: Bloomsbury, 2012.

Martinez, Sylvia Libow, and Gary S. Stager. *Invent to Learn: Making, Tinkering, and
Engineering in the Classroom.* Torrance, CA: Constructing Modern Knowledge
Press, 2013.

Nauss, Jade. "Anchor Archive Zine Library Zines In." *The Coast.* 2014. http://www
.thecoast.ca/halifax/anchor-archive-zine-library-zines-in/Content?oid
=4281983

Part IV

Collaborations, Training, and More

9

Impact through Connection at School: Public Libraries Creating Impact by Bringing Digital Literacies and Maker Skills into the Classroom

Jeroen de Boer

INTRODUCTION

During the spring of 2017, Library Service Friesland (Bibliotheekservice Friesland, or BSF) initiated the project *Impact through Connection at School*, together with Maker Households, a private company led by Ton Zijlstra. This project, a pilot project under the new media literacy policy of the National Library of the Netherlands, took place at an elementary school, the Dr. Algraschool, in Leeuwarden (Coenders, 2016). Other partners were Leeuwarden Public Library (SBMF) and the NHL University for Applied Sciences (NHL).

The experiment centered around helping the group to identify communal issues and situations they would like to change and then to develop ideas and realize them. So that the group "gets" that with various making and other types of machines and instruments, they have the agency and the power to change their surroundings for themselves as a group.

From January 2017 until March 2017, the project team met with the school's team, and then weekly six times with the class of 22 children, aged 10–11. It was loads of fun, and not just for the kids involved. The highest compliment we received was that one of them said, "This is more fun than the annual school trip." Another remarked feeling sorry that all other classes had to work, while they were inventing ideas and making stuff. We pointed out that they too were working very hard but differently and that having fun does not mean you're not working.

AGENCY

Agency, in the definition of Professor Marc Coenders, is:

an ability to work with others in order to expand the solution space by identifying and providing access to resources that others can contribute to when they analyze problems and formulate answers (Coenders, 2016).

Ton Zijlstra sees agency "as a way to succeed in lowering the adoption threshold for existing technologies and techniques. Then any group can recombine those technologies and techniques to create a desired impact in their own contexts and environment" (Zijlstra, 2017). In that sense, it is a working method to get a community on the move, using cheap technologies and open network principles. It seems to apply to library labs in an apt way. It is not restricted to a formal situation, though, but is rather well applicable to the informal nature of library activities. At the same time, it does not mean it is only about play. The pursuit of impact coincides strikingly with the principle of library as a platform, aiming at knowledge development in local communities. However, demands on librarians to guide this process or to help find partners here are high.

The framework that we used has been developed by Zijlstra. The main question we wanted to answer was the following: *How do children adopt new developments and technologies as easily as possible in order to achieve local impact?* The principle is that by using inexpensive technologies and appropriate working methods, the action perspective of children is enhanced. It allows them to have control over the technologies and meaningfully deploy those for themselves and their school or neighborhood.

However, it is not always the case that these technologies are close to the students. In that sense, there is a (digital) literacy gap to bridge. We wanted the pupils to identify a local situation where there is a need and how they can use open technologies and a suited working method to create impact. The starting point is that the tools used are so cheap that they will never hinder the process.

ABOUT FRYSKLAB AND DIGITAL LITERACIES

FryskLab's educational offering seeks to contribute to stimulating the development of digital literacy. In this field, different frameworks exist, but we deliberately chose the approach of Doug Belshaw. He assumes that someone is not just digitally literate because the concept in his view consists of several elements, eight in total. He says:

> It is easy to paint a utopian picture of what can happen when learners connect to information and to one another via digital tools. There's plenty of rhetoric about learning and jobs being available to all through the internet. What is often missing is the recognition of the multiple literacies needed to not only turn desire into action, but even to know what is obtainable (Belshaw, n.d., p. 39).

According to Belshaw, the degree of literacy is dependent on the extent wherein users can remix different literacies (he deliberately used the plural form). They also depend on the context in which they are used. In his book, he illustrates this with a trivial example of an 11-year-old being able to draw a graph when sitting in a mathematics classroom—but not straight afterward in his history classroom (Belshaw is a former history teacher).

Although Belshaw does not specifically link digital literacies with librarianship or maker education, this connection is made by Swedish librarian Åke Nygren (2014), working at Stockholm public library. He devised a way to associate Belshaw's theory with librarianship. Nygren put together eight maker boxes, each one having a link with one of Belshaw's literacies. Each box consists of a piece of open technology (for instance a Raspberry Pi, wearables, a 3D printing pen, or a link to Mozilla software), but it does not come with a manual. During so-called Maker Parties (conducted in 2016), a concept developed by Mozilla, librarians have to find out how the content of the boxes works and, most important, how they link to the different literacies and how all this connects to modern-day librarianship. Learning by doing in its purest form.

ROLE OF THE LOCAL LIBRARY AND LIBRARIANS

The backbone of the project is the objective that the local libraries and librarians facilitate this process from beginning to end. This means the project approach is extremely intensive. It is important that it is not about an individual action perspective or just that of a whole group but that the action perspective of individuals is embedded in a group or social context: How do I strengthen my school and, by that, myself?

In that sense, it fits very well with the task that Leeuwarden Public Library must fulfill in the next couple of years: Because of a decreased number of local branches in the neighborhood, the library should manifest itself by means of so-called *connection points*. This process is ongoing at this moment, and the Agency method could possibly serve as a fitting approach not only in a school setting but also on a neighborhood level and with other focus groups. In the spring of 2017, we want to test this idea with a group of adults in the same area as the school, in a project that will also be funded by the National Library of the Netherlands, as part of their innovation program.

The desired outcome of both projects is twofold. First, it hopefully leads to a process that results in a solution and thus impacts the participants involved. For us, this redefines the role of the library, beautifully written down by David

Lankes: "We too often have accepted the role of libraries as an answer to access instead of an agent of impact" (Lankes, 2017).

In both cases, we also will provide a toolkit that captures the process systematically, so that it can also be used at other schools or neighborhood settings. This toolkit will become available for free for all Dutch public libraries.

JANUARY–MARCH 2017: WORKING IN SCHOOL

We visited the Dr. Algraschool six times. During these sessions, we went through the schedule of the Agency Map:

Session 1 (January 25): A group discussion about the children's environment, things they would like to change, ideas for making things they had. This resulted in a physical "wall of ideas" in the classroom, ordered from "looks less hard to do" to "looks harder to do." We also discussed the idea of robotics with the children and showed them a potential example of an 11-year-old boy who needed a prosthesis for his hand and who chose the e-NABLE prosthesis (2017), mainly because it was cool and could be printed in the colors of his favorite soccer team, Bayern München. This really resonated with the pupils and ignited a discussion about fairness and the way money "works": Why are some prostheses so expensive if you can also have one for a fraction of the costs?

Session 2 (February 1): Getting to know maker machines (3D printers, laser cutter, electronics, etc.) by bringing the machines into the classroom and parking the FryskLab mobile FabLab out front. Children were taught how to work with Tinkercad, an online 3D modeling platform to create 3D designs. They were also able to experiment with littleBits, an open source library of modular electronics that snap together with small magnets for prototyping and learning. This gave them an idea on how to get started with their own ideas.

Session 3 (February 8): Getting to know programming by using micro:bit, the microcontroller invented by the BBC in 2015, which is becoming available in the Netherlands and Iceland in 2017. All the children got one to keep personally as well. Some pupils who already had some coding experience, for instance with Mindcraft or Scratch, were quickly becoming coaches for the other kids.

Session 4 (February 15): Diving deeper into the idea now that they have a notion of what is possible with the machines and material available, using a canvas to think about what the idea solves, whom it is for, what part of the idea to zoom in on, and who in their own social network could help them realize the problem.

Session 5 (March 8): Building prototypes, again with the FryskLab truck parked outside. We also put together a group of pupils who became the project's journalists. They got to know WordPress and learned how to use tablets to make videos and take pictures to include in their online journal.

Session 6 (March 13): Building prototypes and presenting results to each other. Some of the finalized projects included plexible phone covers for phone types that aren't otherwise available, a way to look under water, an Arduino-powered classroom MP3 player for audiobooks, games, computer-controlled door locks, a candy machine, a robot to counteract bullying, Web sites documenting the process, and a money system for the school.

The team responsible for supervising was different each session. Because we could not foresee what would be expected, the team needed to be flexible in the next session. In this sense, we really felt like librarians: taking note of what the pupils needed and trying to find a solution.

GENERATING AND SELECTING THE IDEAS

Generating ideas by the pupils marked the beginning of the project. In a two-hour session with the pupils, each of them was provided with a set of sticky notes to patch their ideas on. Those were then put up on a wall in the classroom (and stayed there for the entire project): a wall of ideas.

The ideas were arranged by the level of feasibility, from easy to hard. It soon turned out that the pupils in thinking about their wishes, coupled with technology, rapidly narrowed this down to making robots. The idea of what a robot is was directly linked to a humanoid figure, which is useful or fun for you: a cleaning robot, a cuddling robot, or a cleanup robot. We quickly had to tell them that the realization of such a robot would not be feasible, at least in this project.

Ton Zijlstra said:

> When we look at making, we see how it is different from what was before, how all of a sudden "anyone" can do things that took specialized machines and factories earlier, and how that changes the dynamics of it all. The children don't see it that way, because they don't have that history. Although that history is the source of our own fascination it is not the fascination you can confer to the children, as it is by definition a meaningless comparison to them (Zijlstra, 2017, para. 20).

We also didn't succeed in our original plan to bring the group to defining one or a few projects that were less person focused and more group focused (except for the kid that designed a currency system for the school) and then selecting parts of them on which individuals or small groups could work. It seems we would need to spend more effort in the run-up to the cycle of sessions to do that properly. We also got this feedback from the group teacher, Annarein Dijkhuis. After the project, she said:

> In the beginning I found it hard to define the substantive purpose and ultimate goal of the project. I felt involved, but on the days itself I wasn't able to help the pupils, because my knowledge about programming or a question about the steps to take to arrive at a final product wasn't sufficient.

However, we gathered some wonderful ideas from the pupils: a device to see underwater (thought up by two classroom friends who shared a love for fishing), flexible cases for obscure cell phones, and a device that automatically turns the pages of a book. Also an idea that did not require a technical solution: a private money system for the school. This last idea resulted from a discussion with the children about value and fairness and about the open source prosthesis: How do money and a money system actually work? Another question that arose: Why shouldn't any kid who needs a prosthesis have access to a reliable and cool aid?

GETTING FAMILIAR WITH THE POSSIBILITIES OF MAKING AND CODING

We used two sessions to let the kids get acquainted with low-cost technology. In the first session, they went to work with 3D designing and 3D printing. For this, we used the FryskLab truck, and we also set up an instant maker space in the classroom. In the truck, they also encountered the laser cutter, as well as equipment such as littleBits. The design task consisted of designing something that was related to the ideas they came up with earlier.

In the second session, students worked with micro:bit. The students received their own copies that they could keep well. Using micro:bit, most of the children took their first steps in programming.

Pupils who already had some programming experience quickly turned out to be coaches for the other kids. After this session, we sat down with the classroom teacher, Annarein Dijkhuis, and the school principal, Cees Joossen, in which Annarein pointed out: "You really touch some kids. It is like opening the world for them. Teaching computer programming? Another thing to do! But when I see what is happening, I see why it is so important." Two months later, she would say, answering a question about digital literacies in her school:

We are well aware of the fact that digital literacy should play a more prominent role in our school. At this moment it is not clear how this should be implemented though. Groups 7 and 8 [10- to 12-year-olds] do participate in the Week of Media Literacy each year. And a short while ago some teachers went to an information meeting about programming in the classroom. We are certainly aware that there is something to be done.

BACK TO THE IDEAS: WHAT IS POSSIBLE, AND WHAT CAN YOU DO YOURSELVES?

After these two technology sessions, we spent a lesson to reflect on the ideas from the first session. It was important to further define their challenge. They were also asked to think about what would be needed to achieve this. For this, they had to answer some questions. They were also asked to visualize the idea. This was all brought together on one canvas. The questions to be answered were as follows:

1. What do I wish to solve, what do I want to change?
2. To which groups do I belong?
3. For whom do I want to do something? Draw that person.
4. What does this person need?
5. What can I make myself?
6. Who would you like to help you? Think of the groups you mentioned in question 2!

The team used these canvases as a basis to determine what the follow-up would look like. Therefore, a shared Google Drive spreadsheet was used, to which the canvases were uploaded. In this spreadsheet, the team members would assign themselves to a number of projects. It was also identified which materials and knowledge sources would be used. Given the diversity of 11 projects, this preparation was really necessary. For example, for the idea of the school money system, we decided to approach an economics teacher. He would talk with Anna, the girl who came up with the idea, about money systems and what is necessary to make them work.

As an example of the canvas results, here are the results from the project *De Onderwaterkijker* (The Underwater Viewer), an idea from best friends and fishing buddies Jesse and Ezra:

1. What do I wish to solve, what do I want to change?
   Less pollution in nature. Less waste in the water, such as branches, pouches, and cans.
2. To which groups do I belong?
   Soccer team, family, school, drumming, fishing team Jesse and Ezra
3. For whom do I want to do something? Draw that person.
4. What does this person need?
   An Underwater Viewer
5. What can I make myself?
   The device to watch under water with
6. Who would you like to help you? Think of the groups you mentioned in question 2!
   Team members Jeroen and Dragan, our class, and ourselves.

MAKING, MAKING, MAKING

The last two sessions were used to let the students actually create their ideas. The evening before the first session, a number of details were discussed with teacher Annarein. She said some pupils were a bit hesitant about the upcoming sessions. Due to illness or other reasons, they did not have an idea to build upon or simply felt a lack of ownership regarding the project they were working on. So we suggested that maybe those students should take up the role of journalist. This would mean that they learned how to use a CMS (Word-Press) and to work with tablets as a means to gather information. The teacher responded enthusiastically, so we told the class the next day that there still was an important but not yet completed project. When asked who wanted to be a journalist, about six students responded. In this way, a component that initially was not part of the program thus proved a popular addition. In a possible follow-up, it will therefore be a fixed element.

Regarding the project ideas, some children had to accept that we could not realize theirs. In one case, the reason was that the idea was too complex (for instance, a device that automatically expresses thoughts by visualizing them). In another case, it would be technically feasible, but it did not fit within the available time and resources (the Anti-Pestomaat, or Anti Bullying Machine, a device that confronts anyone who bullies with their behavior). In both cases, the children had to jump a hurdle and start with another project. That worked in both cases. In the first case, the idea owner created an Arduino MP3 player for classroom use. In the other one, the pupil devoted herself to the role of journalist.

In the end, a total of 11 projects were taken on by the pupils and the FryskLab team. Almost all of them were realized.

ABOUT THE ROLE OF THE LIBRARY

After completion of the project, both pupils and teacher were asked about the role of the library in the project. For the children, the question was, "What do you think about FryskLab being a project of the library?" Most kids answered they really liked it, but some also found it a little weird. One pupil put it this way: "I find it is very good of the library, because they are doing something different, and everybody likes that." Another student commented, "I think it is a bit weird, because books and programming and 3D printers don't have anything to do with each other."

The teacher answered two questions, the first one being: "Impact by Connection at School is a project of the library. What do you think of the development that libraries deal with these issues? Her answer was:

> I find it extremely valuable for society that the library is becoming much broader than just focusing on motivating people to start reading. The library can reach a large group of people of all ages and is easy accessible for many of them. The library raises questions about social issues and connects different knowledge resources to serve specific audiences.

Answering a follow-up question about whether this fitted her personal image of the library, she responded: "I knew that the library was on this course, but for many of my colleagues it came as a surprise that this was an organized project from the library."

LOOKING BACK AT THE PROCESS

In general, we didn't succeed in our original plan to bring the group to defining one or a few projects that were less person focused and more group focused (except for Anna, who designed the school currency system) and then selecting parts of them on which individuals or small groups could work. The process worked in the sense that we got everyone to make things and to dive deep beyond the initial magic and "Wow!" of 3D printing and laser cutters.

The realization for the children that things take time can be complicated—that it is not magic but actual hard work. Some children literally translated it by saying that waiting for a 3D print took very long. Other children could grasp very well that persistence takes time but eventually can take you anywhere. For example, Anne, the student who worked on the school money system, learned that "all is possible and that if you want to make something you really can." When asked what she was doing differently now than before, she replied: "Believing in myself and that if I want to make something, it is always possible." Asked what made it so much fun, she said: "I liked planning my idea a lot. It made it fun, because you can know everything yourself. The idea is all yours. There are no things that are not allowed".

The principle of cooperation, one of the goals of the project, showed itself as something that the children recognized and was perceived as an added value. One of the questions we asked the kids afterward was: "Were there things that you found difficult to do? What did you do then?" The response of Jesse, one of the two pupils working on The Underwater Viewer, was: "Think of an idea. But when accompanied with Ezra we thought very hard together and then we came to a conclusion." His answer to the question "What did you dislike or less fun? Why?" was: "I didn't really like to think about ideas, because it was only thinking and not doing, but it had to happen." Eventually, however, he saw that it was important, responding to the question "What did you learn?": "That it's hard to think of something and that you must first have a plan before you start something."

When we sent classroom teacher Annarein a survey after the project, she also noticed pupils started to act differently:

> Normally the emphasis in the classroom is especially on reading, language, spelling and math. Not everyone excels in those and I especially saw children excel who not very strong in the above fields. They simply flourished in working with their hands, using creativity, practical insight and considering programming. What I found very nice was to see all students starting at the same level. It was new and challenging for all of them. The "rank", because they know exactly who are weak or strong in learning in the classroom, did not count now. Both strong and weak students found each other in terms of ideas, design and implementation, for instance in the case of the water telescope. Everyone starts at zero. The competences that stood out and which I still see in my pupils are problem solving . . . thinking in small steps . . . see[ing] what is the right order to get results. Nothing is impossible! Also showing perseverance to be able to sort out a problem and wanting to solve it. And communicating and working together to reach a solution.

We learned a lot about doing this project, which was really a pilot. Already pointed out is the fact that the process of really thinking about something and making it takes time. Yes, it is possible to build a robot that does things for you, but it takes a lot of steps in doing so. In that sense, it's also important for us to realize that, for this age group, software is often equated to computers and phones, that it is possible to program things that don't look like computers, and that hard- and software are getting merged more and more (cars, IoT, robots).

Likewise making is mostly connected to hardware, objects, and software. Creating "systems" or "processes" is a novel concept, except for the currency making project. Ton Zijlstra: "*For the pupils challenging systems is like a fish changing the water it swims in*" (Zijlstra, 2017). Similarly for most of the children, their actual environment (the street, the neighborhood, the city, etc.) is also like "water" and was mostly perceived as immutable. Or the ideas were far too gigantic to realize (for instance, building large bridges to make commuting to school faster). Measuring things in your environment and acting on those measurements were notably absent in the ideas.

NEXT STEPS

During the project, the school already indicated that it pays too little attention to digital literacy. They do have ambitions, though. That the library could play a role in reaching their ambitions was initially unknown. Thanks to the project, this idea has changed. The school would like to scale up the project, so that other schools in their school association will be able work with it as well. Looking forward we will consider whether this is possible. Among other things, ideally the conduct of research on digital literacy would be part of it.

REFERENCES

Belshaw, Doug. (n.d.). *The Essential Elements of Digital Literacies*. Self-published. http://digitalliteracies

Coenders, Marc. "Agility in Learning: Space, Direction, and Rhythm." October 7, 2016. https://www.nhl.nl/sites/default/files/bedrijven_en_onderzoek/lectora ten_documenten/inauguratie_marc_coenders.pdf

e-NABLE. "Enabling the Future." July 1, 2017. http://enablingthefuture.org/

Koninklijke Bibliotheek. "The Innovation Council." July 12, 2017. https://www.kb .nl/ob/algemene-programmas/innovatie-openbare-bibliotheken/de-innova tieraad

Lankes, David. "Eulogy for the Information Age: The Future is Impact Not Access." June 26, 2017. https://davidlankes.org/eulogy-for-the-information-age-the -future-is-impact-not-access/

Mozilla. "What Is a Maker Party?" July 13, 2017. https://learning.mozilla.org/en -US/events/

Nygren, Åke. *"The Public Library as a Community Hub for Connected Learning."* August 24, 2014. http://library.ifla.org/1014/

Zijlstra, Ton. "More Fun than Annual Class Trip: Making at School, Some First Observations." March 14, 2017. https://www.zylstra.org/blog/2017/03 /more-fun-than-annual-class-trip-making-at-school-some-first-observ ations/

10

Maker Professional Learning for Educators

Laura Fleming

INTRODUCTION

The maker movement is a global revolution of people, from children to adults, who are driving innovation in manufacturing and even extending into the arts. These are people who are looking at the world, recognizing a problem, and creating a solution rather than just buying things or settling for the world the way it is. The maker movement is not just a global revolution in economics or industry; it is also a global revolution in learning. "The influence of the maker movement can be seen across a broad range of spaces and places under the education umbrella" (Halverson & Sheridan, 2014, p. 498). This includes a wide range of formal and informal learning spaces in K–12 who are affording students the opportunity to be able to take control of their own learning and providing access to the tools to help them do so. Educational stakeholders should seek ways to leverage the maker movement. There is something in this movement for everyone.

"Learning through making reaches across the divide between formal and informal learning, pushing us to think more expansively about where and how learning happens" (Halverson & Sheridan, 2014, p. 498). You do not have to be a STEM (Science, Technology, Engineering, and Mathematics) specialist to be a maker educator. What does a maker educator look like? Such an educator looks like you and me. All educators have the capacity to be maker educators. Anyone who is open to expanding his or her definition of schooling can be a maker educator. I have been an educator in the state of New Jersey for

20 years. I started out my teaching career as an elementary school classroom teacher and, after eight years, transitioned into the role of school librarian. At this point in my career, at various times, I have been the librarian for grades K–12. This experience has given me an invaluable perspective both as a library media specialist and as a maker educator. I know very well the learning outcomes and expectations for students as they progress through all grade levels. In addition, I have collaborated with colleagues across those grade levels as well, giving me a good understanding of the standards, the curricula, and their expectations.

Throughout my career as a school librarian, I have always had a philosophy of a participatory culture running through my libraries. Essentially this has meant that I believe in providing as many opportunities as possible for my students not only to consume information and content but also to have access to the tools, materials, and supplies needed to become creators as well. I believe that schools are filled with creativity, and the challenge for us as educators is cultivating it and harnessing it to its fullest. In all of the libraries I have worked in, my task was to transform them. Yes, this inevitably meant eventually renovating the physical spaces, but, more importantly, it meant transforming the culture of the spaces first. My successes in these areas are what led me to be the Library Media Specialist at New Milford High School.

LIBRARY TRANSFORMATION

In 2013, I was recruited by the then principal of New Milford High School, Eric Sheninger, to help them transform their library. Although Eric was well-known for leading innovative practices at this school, Eric once described their library on his blog as a barren wasteland (Sheninger, 2014). Upon starting at New Milford High School, I realized quickly that we did not have the luxury of a big sum of money to renovate our space, so we were forced to think of creative ways to make changes in our space. Those changes focused not on how the space looked but on transforming the culture of the space. When I first started at New Milford, the library was empty. Even at times when the library should have been bustling with activity, it was bare. No one came in that first day or the first few days.

Thanks to a few core changes, our space went from being completely irrelevant to our school community to a thriving learning metropolis (Sheninger, 2014). The initial changes I made to our library were all in line with harnessing a participatory culture. This included providing as many opportunities as possible for our students to do things and to actively participate in their learning. I attribute the quick turnaround of our space directly to the addition of our makerspace. Our first makerspace station consisted of a rotting orange, one Makey Makey kit, and a handwritten construction paper sign (which I made) that said, "An orange as a space bar . . . what can you make?" It was this one conspicuously placed station that started to draw our students in.

The change in our library happened very organically. This one station caught the attention of passersby in the hallways. I could see teens starting to look into the library as they passed, and, ultimately, it was their curiosity about this sign that drew them in. Greeted simply by my smile and a friendly wave, students made their way over to the orange and, on their own, decided to touch the orange to see what would happen. Each and every time a student would touch the orange, they would gasp and laugh upon seeing the space bar on the computer screen move. These students often, upon leaving the library, would soon return with a group of friends. This pattern continued over the course of the next few weeks, as the rest of our makerspace was put together, until our library was standing room only.

Our makerspace has continued to grow and evolve since 2013, but even today the same vibrant culture runs through our library. Our space has garnered national notoriety, featured on the *CBS Evening News* (Hsu, 2014). Due to the success of our makerspace, I was given the opportunity to write a book on makerspaces titled, *Worlds of Making: Best Practices for Establishing a Makerspace for Your School* (Fleming, 2015). Because of that book's publication, I have had the amazing opportunity to work with schools across the nation on planning and creating makerspaces. Through this work, I have discovered key components to maker professional learning for educators. It has been these discoveries that have shaped my work since the publication of this book.

We can all agree that the traditional professional development system is broken and that receiving credit for so-called seat time does not impact student achievement. We are, however, starting to see conversations beginning to shift to professional learning rather than development or training. "Development and training" connotes that something is being done to you, while learning indicates seeking out knowledge to improve one's practice. Twenty-first-century teachers are encouraged to take control of their own professional learning. School districts are now, more than ever, encouraging teachers to chart the course for their own professional learning. This includes educators being encouraged to seek out both formal and informal professional learning opportunities. Maker professional learning for educators should encompass three critical components: *Planning and Creating Meaningful Makerspaces, Shifting Pedagogy and Practice, and Leveraging the Digital Space.*

PLANNING AND CREATING MEANINGFUL MAKERSPACES

Perhaps the most significant discovery I have made in this area has been the importance of professional learning that focuses on the process of properly planning a makerspace. I see far too many educators skipping this step and instead focusing their efforts on learning skills themselves, such as coding and programming, or just bypassing maker professional learning altogether and instead just purchasing makerspace items they see other people buying. Not taking the time to properly plan a makerspace is a critical oversight. Many educators who skip this step are often left wondering why their spaces have not taken off or why their once vibrant spaces have fallen flat.

STEM and makerspaces can have a symbiotic relationship, however, STEM is not always what is best for a school's makerspace, and, in fact, makerspaces do not have to be about STEM at all. I define a makerspace as a metaphor for a unique learning environment that encourages tinkering, play,

MAKERSPACE PLANNING

Makerspace Planning Process (Courtesy of Laura Fleming).

and open-ended exploration for all (Fleming, 2015). Taking time to learn how to properly plan this kind of space helps educators to uncover spaces that are unique, vibrant, and sustainable for their individual school communities rather than something that is trendy or replicated from one school community to the next. Focusing on professional learning in this space will guarantee educators that their space is not only vibrant for the here and now but that their spaces will also be sustainable into the future.

Proper planning of a school makerspace begins with the voice of the learners. Taking time to understand the needs, wants, and interests of your students will help to ensure that your makerspace is the student-driven learning environment we want our spaces to be. Proper planning also consists of making connections to standards, curricula, programs, and offerings within individual school communities. Proper planning also gives your makerspace relevance to what is happening in the world by making connections to global trends and best practices. Synthesizing this data helps educators develop themes for their spaces that are the most meaningful and relevant to their school communities, in addition to helping them make meaningful decisions about how to best to support their themes, which could include purchasing resources, materials, and supplies. (See figure.)

It is important to note too that, even with proper planning, makerspaces are never finished or complete. They are always a work in progress. Revisiting the planning process will help your makerspace grow, evolve, and stay current. My experience has been that educators benefit greatly from professional learning that focuses on proper planning. Although planning is laborious, the more time and effort spent on this component of creating a makerspace ensure that much more that the makerspace is successful.

SHIFTING PEDAGOGY AND PRACTICE

School makerspaces should be driven by students and facilitated by educators. In order to ensure that the needs of students are being met, maker professional learning should reflect the new pedagogy that the maker movement in schools demands. Many educators feel uncomfortable with the idea of makerspaces because it pushes them beyond their own comfort zones. However, it is important for educators to understand that they are creating spaces that work best for their students and that they do not have to be experts at everything in their makerspace. While having a certain maker skill set can come in handy, educators often seek out only professional learning that equips them with maker skills, when, in fact, not being an expert creates an opportunity for your students to take control of their own learning and for educators to have the opportunity to learn right beside their students. This allows students to be able to see their own teachers as learners too, which can be an invaluable lesson.

Makerspaces are rooted in experiential learning, or "learning by doing." An inextricable component of experiential learning is reflection. Learning in a makerspace is an iterative process that is utterly dependent upon reflection and upon building further learning on experiences, thereby leading to more experiences. Reflecting on their making is something our students can do independently, or it can be facilitated. As educators, we need to find and create opportunities for students to reflect, share, and celebrate their makerspace experiences. As vital as this is to the success of our learners, it is equally crucial that we as educators take the time to reflect as well. Teaching is a reflective practice. Often we associate the idea of reflection as something that comes after the fact, but maker professional learning should actually begin with reflection. Taking the time to reflect on our own schooling experiences and on ourselves as learners will help us gain a deeper understanding of the role a makerspace can play for our students. Drawing on personal experiences can help tap into the vast possibilities of what makerspaces can be.

Maker educators understand the importance of students having a growth mindset in a makerspace. We want our students to know that makerspaces are safe learning environments in which they can take chances, step outside their comfort zones, and even fail. Sometimes as a result of those failures, we become our most innovative. It is equally important, though, that maker professional learning instills that same mindset in the educators who are planning, creating, and rolling out makerspaces.

Makerspaces are never complete. They are always a work in progress—growing, evolving, and taking shape. Reflecting on the successes and challenges of a makerspace can help guide your decision making and allow you to make any necessary changes. Maker educators should revisit the Makerspace Planning Process as a means for reflection. Reevaluating the needs of your students, curricular connections, and what is happening in the world might cause educators to keep existing themes in their makerspace, drop irrelevant themes, adopt new themes, or put some themes on the backburner.

Maker professional learning should not be seen as simply training. Educators should be immersed in their maker experiences, and learning should be inquiry driven. Professional learning should model the experiences we want our students to have in our makerspaces. Best practices related to inquiry-based learning allow educators to create the conditions to inspire learners to take risks and innovate. Maker professional learning needs to equip teachers with the tools and strategies they need to allow their learners to flourish, grow, and ultimately to be great.

LEVERAGING THE DIGITAL SPACE

Educators never stop learning, nor should they. "We live in a world in which learning—including teacher learning—can occur anytime and anywhere" (Murray & Zoul, 2015, p. 66). This just-in-time learning is available 24/7, therefore keeping our knowledge base fresh and current. Thanks to mobile devices, educators have access to professional learning right in their pocket. Those devices, along with social media, have made it easier than ever to learn and to share and collaborate with other professionals outside their school and even around the globe.

Educators who strive to become maker educators can use the digital space to tap into diverse strategies and perspectives and to learn with a community of like-minded educators, beyond the four walls of their schools. For some educators, this might be done through Twitter; for others, it might be Facebook or Snapchat or blogs. In other cases, it might be attending a webinar. Podcasts are also an effective means of professional learning. My colleague, educator Travis Lape, and I once hosted a makerspace radio show on the BAM! Radio Network called *Movers & Makers*, whose sole purpose was to expand the boundaries of what professional learning can be for maker educators. The topics of our show included the things we hold most sacred in the professional learning of a maker educator: exploring the maker mindset, breaking down barriers to learning with making, how best to nurture open-ended exploration, unconventional makerspaces, breaking down barriers to learning with making, giving up control as a maker educator, the maker movement from a national perspective, expanding your vision of makerspaces, overcoming the challenges of learning by doing, inside tips on starting and running a makerspace, helping students learn with the head, the heart, and the hand.

Often, professional learning in the digital space is informal in nature and therefore, in many cases, *free*! For me, I stay current on maker practices via Twitter. Specifically, I monitor specific hashtags, such as #makerspace and #makered. I also try to give back to my professional learning network (PLN) by posting maker-related information, with links to resources and my own hashtag, #worldsofmaking. Maker educators should choose platforms that work best for them and connect with educators they can learn from and share best practices.

Maker professional learning for educators is critical in the process of creating great makerspaces. Even those educators who realize this often struggle with finding meaningful opportunities that fit into their busy lives. After hearing this from so many educators, I launched the Worlds of Making Digital Academy (worldsofmaking.teachable.com). The idea behind the Academy is to be able to provide affordable, online, self-paced professional development, allowing for anytime/anywhere maker professional learning! The goals of the courses in the Academy include the things that I hold most sacred in relation to maker professional learning, including:

- Planning, creating, and launching a makerspace in a school, library or classroom.
- Choosing the materials and supplies that will best support a makerspace.

- Supporting a makerspace on any budget.
- Setting up a physical makerspace.
- Effectively managing and facilitating a makerspace.
- Unleashing student creativity.
- Establishing a culture of making.
- Making across content areas.
- Transforming learning spaces to foster making, creativity, and collaboration.

I authored a few courses at the Academy, but courses also have been authored by valuable members of my professional learning network, helping to bring in other voices and perspectives in addition to my own. The courses that are offered are perfect for all makerspace stakeholders, including PK–12 classroom teachers, school library media specialists/librarians, STEM educators, tech integration teachers, educational technology teachers, and school leaders, and they are geared toward those who don't have a makerspace but who want one or to those who do have makerspace but are looking to improve theirs. When educators purchase a course, it is theirs forever. They can complete the courses when they can and when they want to. In addition, they are able to progress through the courses at their own pace! Despite this professional learning being digital, the course authors are always available to support educators along the way.

New forms of professional learning require new forms of acknowledging that learning. Therefore, upon completion of each online course, educators have the opportunity to earn an official Worlds of Making microcredential, in the form of a digital badge, which will allow them to celebrate and display their learning! To earn the microcredential, educators must submit evidence, in various forms, that demonstrates their learnings. Through built-in metadata, each badge tells the story of the maker educator's learning. The microcredentials belong to the educators who earn them and help educators tell their complete story and take ownership of their professional learning. Educators may share their microcredential across social media sites, embed them in blogs or Web sites, upload them to resumes, or include them in portfolios, or they can use them in any way that they wish.

CONCLUSION

The maker movement has been a revolution in education, and all educational stakeholders need to find ways to leverage this movement. The creativity and innovation the maker movement fosters will benefit our students both in school and beyond: making advances in modern skills that promote educational equity, bridging the digital divide and gender gap, and allowing us to create a culture of innovation that is sure to benefit entire school communities and better prepare our learners for the world they will be facing.

Through making, you can foster exploration, innovation, and creativity that is both inspiring and empowering to learners; however, the success of our makerspaces fully depends on meaningful maker professional learning experiences for educators. While building your own making skills can be useful for a maker educator, the pendulum needs to swing more toward focusing on professional learning experiences that model the type of learning we want to happen in a makerspace, as well as guide and support educators through the process of planning and creating not just a makerspace but, instead, a *great* makerspace.

REFERENCES

Fleming, Laura. *Worlds of Making: Best Practices for Establishing a Makerspace for Your School*. Thousand Oaks, CA: Corwin, a SAGE Company, 2015.

Halverson, Erica Rosenfeld, and Kimberly Sheridan. "The Maker Movement in Education." *Harvard Educational Review 84*, no. 4 (2014): 495–504.

Hsu, Cindy. "New Milford H.S. Students Explore New Ways of Learning with Library's 'Makerspace.'" *CBS New York*. February 27, 2014. http://newyork.cbslocal .com/2014/02/27/new-milford-h-s-students-explore-new-ways-of-learning -with-librarys-makerspace/

Murray, Thomas C., and Jeffrey Zoul. *Leading Professional Learning: Tools to Connect and Empower Teachers*. Thousand Oaks, CA: Corwin, a SAGE Company, 2015.

Sheninger, E. "Creating Our Own Unique Learning Environments." #DigiLead. February 23, 2014. http://esheninger.blogspot.com/2014/02/creating-our-own -unique-learning.html

11

Shared Spaces and Makerspaces: A Public Library and School Library Partnership

Roxanne Spray and Melissa Crenshaw

Most librarians would agree that there are tremendous benefits to students when school librarians and public librarians collaborate. Indeed, many of the articles in the past few years of *School Library Journal* and other publications featured or recommended collaborations between school libraries and public libraries. The benefits to students were clear: access to larger collections (Barak, 2015; Bengel, 2013), opportunities to interact with nationally known authors (Keasler, 2016; Murvosh, 2013), and access to the public library's databases for school project research (Bengel, 2013). Some of these benefits are realized with a library card drive and teaching students how to request books and access databases on the public library Web site. This is beneficial for students, but it is not the kind of collaboration that the articles were advocating, though it is a good first step. The challenges to a collaboration that goes beyond a yearly library card drive are complex: coordinating work schedules, getting release time to visit schools on a regular basis, and coordinating with teachers on times for students to come to the library or times for librarians to come to classes. The keys to making these kind of partnerships work are twofold: (1) a shared belief from all stakeholders that a school and public library partnership is worthwhile and (2) clear and consistent communication. Fortunately, for the students at Ware Shoals High School and the patrons of the Ware Shoals branch of the Greenwood County Public Library, we have both.

OUR SHARED SPACE: THE WARE SHOALS COMMUNITY LIBRARY

Although the Ware Shoals library is a branch of the Greenwood County Public Library system, the sign on the side of the building reads "Ware Shoals Community Library" because we are more than a small local branch. Our library is both a public library and a high school library. Melissa Crenshaw is the Ware Shoals branch manager of the Ware Shoals library, and Roxanne Spray is the school librarian for Ware Shoals High School.

We are a truly blended community library: We have one circulation desk: Roxanne sits on the side closest to the high school, and Melissa sits on the side closest to the front door where public patrons come in. We frequently help each other's target populations. Roxanne can help public patrons if Melissa is with another patron, and Melissa can help students if Roxanne is with a class. Our collections are merged on the shelves, but we maintain two circulation systems: one for the resources purchased by the school district and one for the resources purchased by the county library system. High school students can check out public-owned materials if they have a public library card, and public patrons can check out high school books. We even have an informal interlibrary loan system with the district middle school. We do a library card drive at the beginning of each school year, and the middle school librarian teaches the students how to look up books using the library Web site. Middle school students can then request books from the county library— usually via an e-mail from the middle school librarian—and the books go over to the middle school through the school district interdistrict mail delivery. They are returned the same way. This outreach program ensures that upcoming ninth graders are already well versed in library policies and have cultivated a habit of using the library.

If you are curious about how a public library and public school circulate their books together, here is how it works. Students can tell whether a book they want is a public library book either by looking at the bar code or by asking us. County bar codes are located inside the back cover, right above the date due pocket, and have "Greenwood County Library" above the bar code. High school books have the bar code on the front cover of the book and have "Ware Shoals High School." We also put a purple star on the spine label as a visual signal that the book is a high school book.

If students want a Greenwood County book and do not have a library card, we hold the book for them and give them a library card application. They fill it out, have it signed by a parent or guardian, and, when they bring the form back, we enter them into the system, give them a card, and check out the book. If they bring back their application promptly, they just have to wait 24 hours to get the book they want. Since we hold the book for them, not having a card is not a risk for not getting a book they want. Our catalogs are not merged, so if they are looking up a book, they know who owns it based on which catalog they are looking in.

Our library did not start out as a blended library. More than 20 years ago, community members noticed that the high school library and the public library were outgrowing their physical spaces. The idea to merge the two libraries was novel for that time, and the process to get approval and funding was complex;

it involved lawyers, the school board, the state department of education, the legislature, and scores of private donors who believed in the project. Once the funding and approval were in place, construction began in 1998, and the building was dedicated in March 1999. The new building was attached to the high school by a breezeway, and a separate parking lot for public patrons was installed next to the faculty parking area for the high school.

Our physical space is what you might expect from a blended library. Approximately 70% is one large area that patrons see when they walk in: the library collections (picture books, juvenile fiction and nonfiction, graphic novels, young adult fiction, audiobooks, biographies, nonfiction, reference, class sets, book club kits, and the South Carolina collection), computers, a laptop charging cart, a mobile Promethean ActivPanel board, and tables for group and individual work. The other 30% includes a workroom behind the circulation desk; a tiny break room with a refrigerator, sink, and table; the public bathrooms; and a hallway that leads to two large meeting rooms. One of the rooms is used mostly for school meetings, such as faculty meetings, and the other is used for community functions and school board meetings. They are both equipped with projection equipment: a screen/projector combination in one room and a Promethean ActivPanel in the other.

At first, there was considerable resistance to the plan of merging the two libraries. Some community members were uneasy about students and public patrons inhabiting the same space during school hours. The counterargument was that they shared the same space after school when they were both at the grocery store or the gas station (for example). Our policy on that matter is that students and public patrons do not intermingle during school hours. We have had no issue with students and public patrons in the same room at the same time. Public computers are on one side of the library, and student computers are on the other. We have clear lines of sight from the circulation desk, and our policy has been in place long enough that our public patrons are familiar with it, and students who are new to the district are briefed on the policy during library orientation the first week or so of school. Despite the initial resistance, we have not had any issues with our two populations.

One reason our system works as well as it does is that Ware Shoals is small enough for us to get to know most of our patrons. It is a small, rural town situated on the banks of the Saluda River in South Carolina. A textile mill and hydroelectric plant were catalysts for the growth of the town, but Ware Shoals' population is much smaller now than it was before the mill closed in 1984.

Multiple generations of families have matriculated through Ware Shoals Schools; in fact, many of our students enjoy finding their parents and grandparents in the library's collection of yearbooks. Melissa's children are Ware Shoals graduates, and Roxanne's daughter is a student in the district. Melissa is active in the community, substituted and volunteered in the school system before becoming the branch manager, and has been the branch manager for ten years. Before becoming the high school librarian, Roxanne was the librarian at the primary and middle schools and, as a result, is a familiar face to most of the students currently in Ware Shoals District 51 who are in second grade or higher.

Perhaps the biggest factor for the success of a blended public and high school library is Melissa Crenshaw herself. In the ten years that she has been the branch manager, she has developed the library into a fixture of town life, and she and the high school librarians have worked closely together to make sure that students feel welcome using the library and library resources. Every month, two books clubs meet, and there is a weekly knitting and crafting meeting on Tuesday evenings. She works with the main branch to bring a nationally known author and storyteller to speak with the public and the high school students each year. Melissa has an adult coloring group that meets monthly, she does outreach with homeschooling organizations, and she has a robust summer program that includes a book club for adults, movies, game afternoons, a magician, and two end-of-summer reading parties—one for older patrons and one for children. She has also hosted evening concerts, family game nights, and has a yearly Art Gala. All of these events were promoted to the school community as well. By the time Roxanne became the high school librarian, the school/public partnership idea was running smoothly and was ingrained in the community and among the students as a successful venture.

OUR SHARED SPACES: PROGRAMS FOR HIGH SCHOOL STUDENTS

In addition to the public programs that Melissa hosts, we also host week-long lunchtime activities for high school students during Teen Read Week and Teen Tech Week. During these weeks, students are invited to bring their lunch to the library and participate in programs. Common activities were book talks, hooking up the Wii to the big-screen TV (and later the Promethean board), and "retro game" days.

The conversation that led to our makerspace program happened when we were setting up the duct tape art station for one of the Teen Read Week activities. We began talking about the craft-based programs as temporary makerspaces. That led to a conversation about what makerspaces are, what they could be, and how we could create such a program in Ware Shoals. We also talked about creating activities for our teens that took place throughout the school year instead of limiting them to Teen Tech Week and Teen Read Week.

One of the challenges of implementing a makerspace program for our high school students was timing—when to host the program. Freshman, sophomores, and juniors do not have free periods (we do not have a study hall), and if seniors have completed enough credits by their senior year, do not have a full day of classes; they either come in late or leave early. Additionally, many of our students ride the bus to and from school, and we did not want to plan activities that excluded those students from participating. The one constant was lunch; therefore, all of our programs targeted to high school students take place during lunch. That was complicated enough for a high school librarian, but it becomes even more challenging when merging a public library schedule with a high school schedule. The only day Melissa's schedule allowed her to be in the library during both high school lunches was Tuesday: thus the creation of Teen Tuesdays. Both of us purchase the materials we used for our programs. We do not have a hard-and-fast rule for who pays for what; the funding works itself out.

Our Tuesday programs did not start out as Makerspace Tuesdays. The 2015–2016 school year was both the first year of Teen Tuesdays and the year that Roxanne was focused on growing the graphic novel collection. So the first Tuesday of the month was the graphic novel club, the second Tuesday was a Writing Club, the third Tuesday was a book club, and the fourth Tuesday was Makerspace Tuesday. All of the Tuesday ideas—with the notable exception of Makerspace—were spectacular failures, mostly due to outside circumstances, although we could have done a better job of promoting them. We said earlier in the chapter that our public library and school library partnership worked well because we knew our patrons. The problem we had that first year of Teen Tuesdays was not knowing enough about the patrons we assumed we were targeting with the graphic novel club, the writing club, and the book club.

Graphic Novel Club

Many of our students love graphic novels and, when given the chance, enjoy talking about their favorite characters and series. Melissa led the students who attended in creating their own graphic novel. This is another way in which the public and school partnership benefited students: Roxanne is not an artist, but Melissa was able to show them ways to get started. The outside circumstance that we could not control is that many of our graphic novel fans were friends with one another, and lunchtime was the only time that they could socialize because they were in different classes. Our graphic novel club fizzled out.

Creative Writing Club

Several of our students were engaged in creative writing projects, and they were happy to talk with us about the plot and offered to let us read what they were writing. We thought a writing club would be an excellent opportunity for them to have a peer editing circle where they could get feedback on their creative projects. The major flaw in this plan was that while the students were happy to share their creative projects with us because they trusted us, they did not trust their peers. Our writing club fizzled out.

Book Club

The book club was the least successful of all. Our first meeting was an excellent discussion about books and genres and what we each liked about what we were reading. Unfortunately, several of the people who came to that first meeting failed to get along socially. Everyone was polite because they knew that was what was expected in the library, but no one came back. Our book club fizzled out after the first meeting.

Students Working Together to Create 3D Snowflakes (Photo courtesy of Roxanne Spray).

Makerspace Tuesdays

Fortunately for us, our first Makerspace Tuesdays *were* successful. We chose duct tape art for the first makerspace meeting because it was popular during Teen Read Week and Teen Tech Week, and several of our students had asked to do it again. Our students had fun, and the library became very busy on the fourth Tuesday of the Month.

We defined makerspaces very loosely during that first year. Legos® were popular with our students, and we hosted Lego Tuesdays several times. Duct tape art continued to be popular, and we bought a book of duct tape crafts for the students to try. Coloring for adults was getting a lot of attention in the mainstream news and social media, so we included coloring and drawing in the makerspace rotation. During November, we expanded Makerspace Tuesday to Makerspace Week, and our students created 3D snowflakes using some excess photo paper and craft paper we happened to have in the library. We hung the snowflakes from the ceiling tiles during December, and students took them home when they left for winter break.

One of the most popular things we did were yarn crafts. Melissa is very good at knitting and crocheting, so we bought yarn, knitting needles, crochet hooks, and round looms and had several yarn craft Tuesdays in the library. One of our seniors chose knitting for her senior project and led two lunchtime classes on using the looms to make hats. One lunch period is not enough time to finish a hat, so the students in her class spent every lunch period in the library eating and looming until they finished their projects.

OUR SHARED SPACES: REFINING AND EXPANDING

Although it was disheartening that 75% of our teen programs that first year were less than successful, we were thrilled that our makerspace offerings were so successful with our students. Once they moved past their surprise that we were doing, as one student put it, "nonbook things" in the library, they were happy to participate. Barron and Barron (2016) offer seven reasons why students respond so well to maker programs, but the three that are the most applicable to today's students are that maker projects get students on their feet and the blood moving, making engages the brain from the blood flow, and making encourages community. It is counterintuitive, but it can be exhausting to sit still for an entire class. Our teachers do a good job of varying instructional methods, often combining mini lectures, group work, and independent work in the same class period. But for most classes at most schools, students are doing most of their work at a desk. Coming to the library and moving around while making a project does indeed get students' blood flowing. Watching them concentrate and help each other as they learn a new skill or become more proficient with practice is evidence of their brain boost. There is also a sense of community when the same group of students comes to the library to make snowflakes or to knit hats.

We wanted to build upon the momentum of the first year to expand our makerspace offerings: We carried over several projects from the year before, such as duct tape crafts, Legos, knitting looms, and the ever popular choose-your-own-project day where students can look through our supplies and create projects of their own.

We also reorganized our Teen Tuesday programs based on what we had learned the previous year:

First Tuesday—Teen Advisory Board: We talk with students about upcoming projects (like makerspace projects for that month) and solicit ideas for things they would like to do.

Second Tuesday—Teen Coloring: This was so popular—and so easy to set up—that we pulled it out for a day of its own.

Third Tuesday—Makerspace Tuesday: We moved up makerspaces to the third Tuesday so that if students wanted more time on their projects that month, they could have them. We wanted to move by months so that monthly reports were easier to write.

Fourth Tuesday—Kahoot! in the Library: Kahoot! is a Web-based trivia game that has had a popularity surge in classrooms as a form of test review or bell-ringer work. We have a trivia board in the library, and the Kahoot! games come from that month's trivia facts.

STUDENT FAVORITES: COLORING AND CROCHETING

Our Teen Coloring Tuesdays program is very popular, and the setup is minimal—pull out the coloring sheets, crayons, and colored pencils. Our students love it: If there are classes in the library after we have set up the coloring area, multiple students ask to take a copy of the coloring sheets we have set out for that day. One of the best parts about our coloring program happened by accident. On one of our Coloring Tuesdays, the library got very busy after lunch, and we did not have a chance to put our coloring supplies back until the end of the day. During the moments when we had time to look up and take a breath, we noticed that students who finished their work early asked their teacher if they could color for the rest of the period. Students who came individually asked to take coloring sheets back to class with them. Students whose classes came in for checkout asked to color after they found their books. By the end of that crazy day, when the supplies still had not been put away, students who were waiting on rides to pick them up were coloring quietly.

This was an activity that obviously resonated with our students. Melissa bought a large-size coloring book with 12 prints on extra thick paper, so we could build on the popularity of our coloring program and create a community art project. We cleared a group worktable, put up a tabletop sign about a Community Collaborative Art Project, and set out crayons and colored pencils. Our goal was to put the finished pieces in Melissa's Art Gala in a special Community Art section, and we assumed we might have three or four finished pieces.

Rather than three or four, our students colored every sheet in that book, a few minutes at a time, in three months. They colored when they arrived early and waited for the first bell. They colored after school while they waited for sports practice to begin. When they finished work early, they came down to the library with passes that specifically said they had permission to color for the rest of the period. One of our High School 101 teachers brought her students to the library for a Fun Friday reward for weeks of good behavior in class. The reward they had chosen as a group was to come to the library to read and color.

This was our most low-key makerspace; we barely did more than set out the materials, and our students did the rest. As a result of our school and public partnership, our students are learning that collaborative artwork is valuable and worthy of display. Additionally, we have been promoting the Art Gala to our students and inviting them to submit their work. During the Gala opening night, they have the opportunity to talk to older artists in the community, see their work displayed, and expand their own artistic horizons.

Another makerspace project that grew beyond a once-a-month activity was crocheting. Melissa taught our first and second lunch students a chain stitch and the single crochet stitch, and several of them got very interested in the project. But for four of our students, our crochet makerspace was not limited to Tuesdays. They came to the library nearly every day in February to work on their projects—sometimes with lunch and sometimes without. That one crochet makerspace project has evolved to a daily lunchtime crochet club. It is an excellent example of the sixth benefit of community in makerspaces discussed by Barron and Barron (2016). The students began asking to take their projects home and work on them there too. Our crochet makerspace has also spread to a classroom. One of our teachers is teaching a life skills class, and Melissa is teaching her students how to crochet. She started out by visiting their classroom and teaching the basic chain stitch, and, for the second lesson, the students visited the library.

CHALLENGES OF TIME, MONEY, AND SPACE

By our own estimation, our makerspace program is an overwhelming success, but it is not without frustrations, and we suspect that our frustrations are similar to others with maker learning spaces in their libraries: time, money, and space. We have had to keep time in the forefront of every makerspace project that we design. Last school year, students had only 30 minutes for lunch; due to that time constraint, we nearly abandoned the project altogether. We made it work by choosing projects that could be completed in

30 minutes or less or projects that had a natural stopping point after 30 minutes and could be stored and picked up later.

This year is even more challenging. Students have 25 minutes for lunch, and by the time they get out of class, go through the line, and walk with their trays to the library, sometimes they have only 15 minutes to complete a project. If students choose to eat first and then come to the library to participate, they often only have 5 to 7 minutes to begin a project. Our third Tuesday of the month schedule for makerspace programs has often evolved to every day of the third week of the month because that is how long it is taking students to finish. Some students do not have the patience for weeklong projects, but those who do invariably have fun.

Issues of funding are familiar issues to schools and libraries, and ours is no different. When we evaluate potential makerspace projects, the ones that make the cut are the ones that require supplies either that we already have or that can be bought very inexpensively. One thing that we are looking forward to doing is more making with electronics, and since our high school will be going 1:1 the next school year, that has real potential. It is exciting to imagine how things will become easier when everyone has a computer and can work on individual projects during and outside of makerspace time in the library. We can help our students with everything from video book trailers to coding with Scratch, and with their own computer, they can work independently or with a partner in the library.

The issue of space is one of the real challenges we are facing in our library. Many maker programs utilize rolling carts or bins or a combination of both. Our shortened maker times have meant that we need a place to store not only maker materials but also student projects between the times that they are actively working on them. It is time for a ruthless weeding and culling of the things in our storage closet, and that is a project we will be undertaking before the end of this school year.

PLANS FOR THE FUTURE

Our biggest plan for the future is to keep our makerspace program a central part of our activities for our students and to keep it relevant and fun. These are some of our overall goals for the program:

> *Maintain our focus on crafts that require hands-on activities*—We enjoy teaching students to knit and crochet not because we think that they will begin making their own sweaters but because, as Root-Bernstein and Root-Bernstein (2013) note, "Arts and crafts develop such skills as observation, visual thinking, the ability to recognize and form patterns, and manipulative ability." When they are crocheting, a dishcloth becomes more than an opportunity to practice the single crochet stitch. It sharpens their thinking skills at the same time.
>
> *Integrate electronic maker projects*—We have been hesitant to incorporate electronic maker projects or to introduce the students to coding languages like Scratch because of the time factor—with our already shortened lunches, simply logging on to a computer that has not created a user's directory structure or saved their login credentials can take all of the time available for electronic projects. Next year,

however, our students will each have their own computers and will likely be logged in when they arrived at the library. That does not solve all of the time problems, but it eradicates the barrier that has stopped us from attempting electronic projects at all. Some of the projects we have wanted to attempt include creating video book trailers and a QR code–based library orientation, where students scan a QR code on their phones and listen to students explaining the different sections of the library instead of watching us explain things.

Go mobile with our maker materials—We would like to take our maker materials to other populations that may not be able to come to the library, such as the Senior Center. There are also mobile opportunities at the Halloween Festival on the square (these would have to be very simple, quick to make crafts) or the annual Catfish Feastival (yes, it is spelled like "Feast" plus "-ival"), which is well attended by the town and surrounding areas.

DO YOU SEE COLLABORATIONS IN YOUR FUTURE?

We will be the first to admit that we do not face the biggest hurdles to a thriving public and school library collaboration. We already have buy-in from the district office, the school board, the county library, the students, and the public. We do not have to manage transportation, and we have very few scheduling difficulties. For those school librarians and public librarians who want to forge a collaborative relationship, here are some things to consider.

The very first thing to do in order to get buy-in from school district personnel and public library directors is to be able to frame your plans in terms of how they will benefit students. In South Carolina, our Department of Education has created a document called "Profile of the South Carolina Graduate" that outlines three categories of skills and competencies that we want South Carolina high school graduates to master before graduation. Makerspace projects incorporate nine of the 13 skill sets listed in that document: creativity and innovation; critical thinking and problem solving; collaboration and teamwork; communication, information, media, and technology; knowing how to learn; self-direction; perseverance; work ethic; and interpersonal skills. Even if your state does not have a similar document, those nine skill sets are critical for success beyond high school, and would be legitimate rationales for a collaborative partnership.

After articulating how a school/public library collaboration will benefit students, the funding needs to be allocated, and the time and place for the projects should be determined. Our lunchtime activities work for us because we do not have to factor in travel time. If the makerspace project is an arts and crafts project, the school's art teacher may welcome the opportunity to incorporate the project into one of the units that is taught. Some maker projects involve numbers and angles; after standardized testing is over, math teachers may welcome the idea of a hands-on project to reinforce the concepts that students have spent the year mastering. Similarly, English teachers may appreciate the opportunity for students to make book trailers of the novels they have read in class that year—but, again, wait until standardized testing is over.

As Melissa says about makerspace projects, "The makerspace is the existence of something yet to be created." That philosophy can also be applied to school and public library partnerships. The potential and possibility exist for rich collaborations, and (like makerspaces), each one should be customized to meet the needs of the patrons. With enough creativity and careful planning, the right time, space, materials, and personnel will eventually fall into place. And, of course, we would welcome anyone who has questions to visit us in Ware Shoals to see our partnership in action.

REFERENCES

Barak, Lauren. "MyLibraryNYC Brings Public Library Services to City Schools, 500,000+ Students." *School Library Journal.* June 24, 2015. http://www.slj .com/2015/06/public-libraries/mylibrarynyc-brings-public-library-services -to-city-schools-500000-k-12-students/

Barron, Carrie, and Alton Barron. "Sevens Surprising Benefits of Maker Spaces." *School Library Journal.* August 2, 2016. http://www.slj.com/2016/08 /technology/seven-surprising-benefits-of-maker-spaces/

Bengel, Tricia Racke. "Libraries with No Bounds: How Limitless Libraries Transformed Nashville Public Schools' Libraries." *School Library Journal.* January 14, 2013. http://www.slj.com/2013/01/programs/libraries-with-no -bounds-how-limitless-libraries-transformed-nashville-public-schools -libraries/

Keasler, Christina. "Working Together: Simple Ways Public and School Librarians Can Collaborate." *School Library Journal.* September 21, 2016. http://www .slj.com/2016/09/programs/better-together-simple-ways-public-and -school-librarians-can-collaborate/

Murvosh, Marta. "Partners in Success: When School and Public Librarians Join Forces, Kids Win. *School Library Journal.* January 1, 2013. http://www.slj .com/2013/01/programs/partners-in-success-when-school-and-public -librarians-join-forces-kids-win/

Root-Bernstein, Robert, and Michele Root-Bernstein. "The Art and Craft of Science." *Educational Leadership 70*, no. 5 (2013): 16–21.

Additional Resources and Reading

BOOKS

Bagley, Caitlin A. *Makerspaces: Top Trailblazing Projects*. Chicago: ALA Editions, 2014.

> A look at makerspaces in public, academic, and school libraries across the United States. Examine nine different makerspaces, along with their successes and challenges, as they implement maker learning spaces in their libraries.

Doorley, Scott. *Make Space: How to Set the Stage for Creative Collaboration*. Hoboken, NJ: Wiley, 2012.

> This book focuses more on an actual space and how it can be used to foster creativity and making. Looking for ways to change your library or classroom? Take a look at this book for unconventional and creative ways to enhance your learning locations. Tools, situations, space studies, and insights are just the beginning of the topics covered in this book.

Egbert, Megan. *Creating Makers: How to Start a Learning Revolution at your Library*. Santa Barbara, CA: Libraries Unlimited, 2016.

> A user-friendly read on creating a "maker mentality" in the library. A monograph that addresses all ages, experiences, and education levels. Particularly useful for those looking to create a maker environment on a limited budget.

Fleming, Laura. *Worlds of Making: Best Practices for Establishing a Makerspace for Your School*. Thousand Oaks, CA: Corwin, a SAGE Company, 2015.

A very hands-on, pragmatic book for practitioners in the field looking to incorporate making and makerspaces in their libraries. Laura's book includes an action plan as well as activities to line up with state and national standards. Easy to use and very practical for the school librarian.

Graves, Colleen, and Aaron Graves. *The Big Book of Maker Space Projects: Inspiring Makers to Experiment, Create, and Learn.* New York: McGraw-Hill Education, 2016.

The Graves duo offers a book packed with easy to follow, simple to use do-it-yourself maker projects. Systematic instructions, as well as images, are offered.

Graves, Colleen, Aaron Graves, and Diana L. Rendina. *Challenge-Based Learning in the School Library Makerspace.* Santa Barbara, CA: Libraries Unlimited, 2017.

Take your maker learning space to the next level with this book. Integrate problem solving, design thinking, empathy building, and much more through this engaging and easy to use book created for the maker librarian and educator.

Hamilton, Matthew, and Dara Hanke Schmidt. *Make It Here: Inciting Creativity and Innovation in Your Library.* Santa Barbara, CA: ABC-CLIO, 2014.

Looking for more case studies of making in libraries? Then this is the book for you. *Make It Here* includes Maker Profiles in each chapter, giving the reader a look into maker learning spaces around the United States.

Hatch, Mark. *The Maker Movement Manifesto: Rules for Innovation in the New World of Crafters, Hackers, and Tinkerers.* New York: McGraw-Hill Professional, 2013.

From March Hatch, who has been with the maker movement from its beginning. This book takes you into the idea of making, what a maker is, ideas behind making, and the maker movement. This book offers an overview of the idea of making, hacking, and fabing.

Kroski, Ellyssa. *The Makerspace Librarian's Sourcebook.* Chicago: ALA Editions, 2017.

Look into makerspaces and technology, delving specifically into the 11 most popular technologies used in makerspaces at the time. Funding, start-up ideas, safety guides, and much more are offered.

Martinez, Sylvia Libow, and Gary S. Stager. *Invent to Learn: Making, Tinkering, and Engineering in the Classroom.* N.p.: Constructing Modern Knowledge Press, 2013.

Written for educators interested in bringing making into their curriculum. This book takes librarians and their peer educators through the process of making in their teaching spaces.

Minow, Mary, Tomas A. Lipinski, and Gretchen McCord. *The Library's Legal Answers for Makerspaces*. Chicago: ALA Editions, 2016.

> Something a little different from the rest of the resources on this list. This particular read takes you through the legal issues that a makerspace can bring into a library. Worth knowing about and definitely a topic to understand as a maker librarian and educator.

Pawloski, Lynn, and Cindy Wall. *Maker Literacy: A New Approach to Literacy Programming for Libraries*. Santa Barbara, CA: Libraries Unlimited, 2016.

> Currently one of the only books available focusing on literacy and makerspaces. A great resource for teen and children's librarians looking to incorporate making and maker activities into their libraries through literacy and technology.

Peppler, Kylie, Erica Halverson, and Yasmin B. Kafai, eds. *Makeology: Makerspaces as Learning Environments*. Abington, United Kingdom: Routledge, 2016.

> If you are looking for a deeper dive with your making, then this is the book for you. Specifically focusing on makers and their "interest-driven learning," this read gives practical tips and ideas for the school librarian and their peer educators.

Preddy, Leslie. *School Library Makerspaces: Grades 6–12*. Santa Barbara, CA: Libraries Unlimited, 2013.

> One of the very first books released on the topic of makerspaces in school libraries. Preddy shares budgets, activities, creations, and more in this easy to follow book. An incredibly useful resource for middle and high school librarians and educators.

Provenzano, Nicholas. *Your Starter Guide to Makerspaces*. N.p.: Blend Education, 2016.

> A very approachable read about integrating making and makerspaces in schools and libraries. Fun and user-friendly, the author gives readers a practical and approachable look at making in education.

Spires, Ashley. *The Most Magnificent Thing*. Toronto ON, Canada: Kids Can Press Limited, 2014.

> A little something different for a book about making. *The Most Magnificent Thing* is a fiction book about a young girl who wants to make something amazing and magnificent. This book would make a good introductory read into making for young people.

Wilkinson, Karen, and Mike Petrich. *The Art of Tinkering*. New York: Simon & Schuster, 2014.

> From San Francisco's Exploratorium Studio, this book looks into what it means to tinker. Delve into the stories of over 150 makers and their individual and extraordinary work in making and tinkering.

ARTICLES

Bowler, Leanne, and Ryan Champagne. "Mindful Makers: Question Prompts to Help Guide Young Peoples' Critical Technical Practices in Maker Spaces in Libraries, Museums, and Community-Based Youth Organizations." *Library & Information Science Research 38*, no. 2 (2016): 117–124.

> Bowler and Ryan look at question prompts to delve into reflection and design in the making process with young people. They specifically look into maker learning locations set in libraries, museum, and other community-based localities. The question prompts guide young people into being more mindful makers. They also can lead to a type of assessment and critical thinking.

Canino-Fluit, Ana. "School Library Maker Spaces: Making It Up as I Go." *Teacher Librarian 41*, no. 5 (2014): 21–27.

> This particular piece offers a well-rounded introduction to making in school libraries. Making and makerspaces are explained. If you are seeking a nice introductory read to the idea of creation and maker learning spaces, this is definitely the one to read. Canino-Fluit provides an approachable article with standard alignment, as well as ideas for launching your own maker club.

Craddock, IdaMae Louise. "Makers on the Move: A Mobile Makerspace at a Comprehensive Public High School." *Library Hi Tech 33*, no. 4 (2015): 497–504.

> For a look at makerspaces without a fixed location, make sure to read Craddock's article on high school students who take their maker activities to local middle and elementary schools. The article discusses the growth of mobile making, the challenges and successes in mobility, and how the mobile program was implemented.

Halverson, Erica Rosenfeld, and Kimberly Sheridan. "The Maker Movement in Education." *Harvard Educational Review 84*, no. 4 (2014): 495–504.

> In this publication, the authors provide a literature review/essay on the maker movement and its role in education. The potential roots of the movement are discussed. Informal and formal education is also a point of conversation in this piece. A very important piece of literature when it comes to the overall idea of making in education.

Peltonen, Marjukka, and Mikaela Wickström. "3D-Prints and Robots Play a Part in My Story. Participatory Learning Action and Content Creation in a Library Maker Space." August 16, 2014. http://library.ifla.org/869/

> In this article/conference proceeding, the authors describe how technologies such as digital filmmaking, animation, robotics, and more were used in their library makerspace. Through an international lens, read about these librarians and how they put together a makerspace as they learned alongside their patrons.

Peppler, Kylie, Adam Maltese, Anna Keune, Stephanie Chang, Lisa Regalla, and Maker Education Initiative. "Survey of Makerspaces, Parts I, II, III." *Open Portfolios Maker Education Initiative* (2015).

> Members of the Maker Education Initiative reached out to a wide range of makers, educators, and librarians in makerspaces of all types. The authors of these three pieces wanted to learn more about where makerspaces were located, the populations served, and the types of activities and programs offered. Each section of the survey report offers information about making in education, the naming of maker learning locations, portfolios, assessment, and much more. A well-rounded and highly useful series of publications.

Range, Ellen, and Jessica Schmidt. "Explore, Plan, Create: Developing a Makerspace for Your School Community." *School Library Monthly 30*, no. 7 (2014): 8–10.

> A very hands-on, approachable article about makerspaces and implementing them in schools. The authors take the reader through making, working with students, support, and building stamina. There is also a great section on finding experts to aid in makerspaces. While we cannot all be the experts in everything, there are always people in our communities, including our students, teachers, and parents, who can help.

Sheridan, Kimberly, Erica Rosenfeld Halverson, Breanne Litts, Lisa Brahms, Lynette Jacobs-Priebe, and Trevor Owens. "Learning in the Making: A Comparative Case Study of Three Makerspaces." *Harvard Educational Review 84,* no. 4 (2014): 505–531.

> While this article does not specifically focus on school libraries, it is such an important piece of literature in the field of makerspaces and education, it had to be included in this list. The authors delve into a comparative case study looking at three makerspaces as learning environments. Using field observations, interviews, and various analyses, they describe how makerspace participants work, build, learn, and create in maker learning spaces.

Small, Ruth V. "The Motivational and Information Needs of Young Innovators: Stimulating Student Creativity and Inventive Thinking." *School Library Research 17* (2014).

> Looking more into the mind of young innovators and creators, Ruth Small writes on the ways that schools can provide more opportunities to make, produce, invent, and discover. Her article specifically delves into a study of the attitudes of young innovators from fourth to eighth grade as they proceed through the process of innovation. More of a "deep dive" into the mind of the young creator and great article in the field of making and creating.

Subramaniam, Mega M., June Ahn, Kenneth R. Fleischmann, and Allison Druin. "Reimagining the Role of School Libraries in STEM Education: Creating Hybrid Spaces for Exploration." *The Library Quarterly 82*, no. 2 (2012): 161–182.

Mega and her fellow authors explore how school libraries can be used as a fusion or cross-location for STEM learning. The school library is the perfect location and the school librarian the perfect person to aid in STEM learning within the school based on the wealth and background of their training. This article further explores that idea.

Williams, Beth Filar, and Michelle Folkman. "Librarians as Makers." *Journal of Library Administration 57*, no. 1 (2017): 17–35.

Williams and Folkman look at the librarian as a maker, what it takes to be a librarian maker, as well as the training involved to be a maker and run a makerspace in a library. Maker training for librarians and the resources available for professional development and preparation are areas not often covered in literature; this article covers that topic well.

BLOGS

Ajima, Josh. "Design, Make, Teach." Blog. 2017. https://designmaketeach .com/

Josh's blog is all about making in the classroom. His blog is part of his personal professional development and a model of the design, make, and share process. He offers demos, presentations, and workshops on 3D printing, technology integration, and professional development. The Design, Make, Teach blog is an extension of his work.

Fleming, Laura. "Worlds of Learning." Blog. 2017. http://worlds-of-learning .com/

As a researcher in libraries, technology, and instruction, I have been interviewing librarians for years. Laura was one of the first professionals whom I started to follow in the field of school librarianship and making. Her blog does not just include information about making (though there is plenty); she shares information about everything in librarianship from coding to digital badges. A blogger well worth knowing, if you don't already.

Graves, Colleen. "Create, Collaborate, Innovate." Blog. 2017. https:// colleengraves.org/

Colleen is an author, blogger, and high school librarian. A maker herself, she loves to write, talk, present, and publish about making and makerspaces in libraries. Her blog is a wealth of information about making. If you search categories, you will find everything from Spheros to accessibility. Her blog is easy to search and has a plethora of ideas for getting started in making or if you are just looking for new ideas.

Make. "Makezine." Blog. 2017. http://makezine.com/blog/

The name in making and maker, Makezine is the place to go. Their blog offers stories, projects, ideas, maker faire locations, and so much more. If you really like what you see, subscribe to *Make* magazine as well. You can never go wrong with having the Make Blog bookmarked on your favorite device or RSS reader.

Rendina, Diana. "Renovated Learning." Blog. 2017. http://renovatedlearning .com/

Diana is a school librarian sharing all of her experience as a maker librarian. She shares every step of any maker process in her library. Images, ideas, practical tips—they are all included in her blog. She is approachable and easy to follow; she has wonderful material on her blog. If you are looking to start a makerspace or if you are just looking for maker ideas, check out Diana's blog.

About the Editor and Contributors

EDITOR

HEATHER MOOREFIELD-LANG serves as associate professor at the University of South Carolina in the School of Library and Information Science. Her research is focused in emerging technologies and their use in education and libraries. Heather is interested in how technologies can further enhance instruction. Her current research focuses on makerspaces in libraries of all types and levels. She has had the honor of being nominated for the White House Champion of Change for Making in 2016. To learn more, see her Web site www.techfifteen.com, visit her YouTube Channel Tech 15, or follow her on Twitter @actinginthelib.

CONTRIBUTORS

STACY BROWN is the 21st Century Learning Coordinator at The Davis Academy in Atlanta, Georgia, where she manages two media centers in a kindergarten prep through eighth grade academic environment. Recognized for facilitating the integration of technology into the curriculum, she leads #MakerMonday for kindergarten prep through fifth grade, teaches a fourth-grade programming and robotics class, developed a fifth-grade entrepreneurship and technology course, and leads teachers' professional development in the area of technology integration. Stacy earned her master's in library and information sciences from Florida State University and her bachelor of arts in English with a minor in French from The University of Texas at Austin. She currently serves on the board for both Atlanta Area Technology Educators and

Savvy Cyber Kids, Inc. and is the winner of the 2016 Marilyn Shubin Professional Service Award. Stacy inspires a thoughtful use of technology, an enthusiasm for reading, and a lifelong interest in learning through both her personal and professional achievements.

IDAMAE CRADDOCK, M.Ed, a 16-year veteran of Albemarle County, is the librarian at the Jackson P. Burley Middle School. Ms. Craddock has spoken at the White House, the Bay Area MakerFaire, MakerEd, and The South Carolina Association of School Libraries. Winner of the Magna Award from the National Association of School Boards, her publishing credits include *Library High-Tech*, *School Library Journal*, and *Knowledge Quest*. The focus of her research is Maker Education and the role of school libraries in the community. Her program has been profiled by *School Library Journal*, Library Media Connection, NPR, and Edutopia. She has a spirited daughter, an understanding husband, and a lazy dog named Peacha.

MELISSA CRENSHAW is a branch manager for the Ware Shoals Community Library. This is her tenth year at Ware Shoals Community Library. Melissa has created and orchestrated numerous community programs involving all age groups. Her focus is creating an enriching environment for her library for which the community can be more connected, informed, and entertained through free access to the resources and programs. Previously in her career, she worked in the school district for nine years, was a Girl Scout leader for ten years, and has written various articles. She has a wonderful husband and two beautiful daughters and has recently welcomed her first granddaughter.

JEROEN DE BOER works at Bibliotheekservice Fryslân (BSF, Leeuwarden, the Netherlands) as Innovation Advisor. He is a strong believer in open technologies and the way libraries can and should learn from maker culture. This is one of the main reasons why Jeroen served on the board of the FabLab Benelux Foundation for the last three years, first as secretary, later as chairman. One of the projects he currently works on is FryskLab, a Mobile Library FabLab (Europe's first). He writes regularly on his personal blog and in professional magazines and gives presentations about libraries, innovation, and makerspaces at (international) library conferences. In 2015, Jeroen was nominated for Librarian of the Year in the Netherlands, in which he was awarded second best. He was also on the Europeana Task Force Public Libraries, focusing on library maker spaces in relation to the (re)-use of cultural heritage content. In his spare time, he is a music afficionado and an avid amateur cyclist.

LAURA FLEMING has been an educator in the state of New Jersey for 20 years. She has been both a classroom teacher and media specialist in grades K–8 and currently as a Library Media Specialist for grades 9–12. She has played a prominent role in education as a writer and speaker and has served as an educational consultant on next-generation teaching methods and tools. Laura cohosts the *Movers & Makers* Podcast and is the author of the best-selling *Worlds of Learning: Best Practices for Establishing a Makerspace for Your School*

(Corwin, 2015). She is also the author of the soon to be released book, *The Kickstart Guide to Making GREAT Makerspaces* (Corwin, 2017).

PHIL GOERNER is the Instructional Librarian at Silver Creek High School in St Vrain Valley. His library, which won Colorado Library of the Year in 2012, is an active place with team teaching, presentations, poetry slams, book clubs, makerspace, and strong academic expectations. Phil is also a University of Colorado at Denver lecturer in the Library Sciences program. He loves technology and learning from his Personal Learning Network on Twitter @pgoerner. He constantly experiments with his makerspace students and loves collaboration, 21st-century skills, innovation, and his hobby of beekeeping!

STACY HAMMER is a second-year elementary school librarian at Battlefield Elementary School in Spotsylvania, Virginia. A Michigan native, she is a graduate of Wayne State University and the University of Michigan. Before earning a School Librarianship Endorsement from Longwood University, she taught middle school English. She loves children's books, kayaking, her two dogs, and Vernor's ginger ale. She lives in Fredericksburg, Virginia, with her husband and their two children.

SARAH JUSTICE is the media specialist at Rosman Middle and High Schools in Transylvania County, North Carolina. She was the 2016 North Carolina School Library Media Association Media Coordinator of the Year. Sarah has worked her way across the state of North Carolina in pursuit of her education. She received her undergrad from Appalachian State University, MLIS, from University of North Carolina Greensboro, and her MAEd IT from East Carolina University. Her passions include reading young adult literature and stalking authors—all to make her a better media specialist since she has to know what to recommend to the students, right? You can follow her adventures on Twitter at @sarahpjustice, Facebook @rosmanmedia, and Instagram @rosmanmedia.

LUCAS MAXWELL grew up in Nova Scotia, Canada, and worked as a fisherman, a door-to-door salesperson, a roof builder, and a stand-up comic before finally settling on being a professional librarian. He worked with teens in the public library for five years and then moved with his family to the UK, where he is currently working as a high school librarian in south London. He is a regular contributor for the Book Riot Web site and can be found on Twitter @lucasjmaxwell.

GINA SEYMOUR is the library media specialist at Islip High School, New York. Gina was awarded the Suffolk School Library Media Association's School Librarian of the Year in 2014, and in 2017 she was named to *Library Journal*'s Movers & Shakers list as a Change Agent. Gina serves on numerous committees for ALA and YALSA and is an adjunct professor at St. John's University. Look for her upcoming book, *Makers with a Cause* (Libraries Unlimited). Gina shares her work, musings, and reflections on her blog GinaSeymour.com and on Twitter @ginaseymour.

ROXANNE SPRAY, MA, MLIS, is the librarian at Ware Shoals High School. This is her third year at the high school and her eighth year as a school librarian. Her passions are educational technology, young adult literature, and creative ways to make the library comfortable and welcoming to her students and patrons. She has learned that makerspaces are a wonderful way to do all three—sometimes at the same time. In her past professional lives, Roxanne was a technical writer, bookseller, college English instructor, writing center tutor, and professional student. She has a loving and supportive husband, an inquisitive and delightful daughter, and three crazy cats.

JENNIFER TAZEROUTI is a National Board Certified Teacher-Librarian who has been working with adults, children, and teens for over 23 years. She received her Master of Library and Information Science from the University of South Carolina, and her Master of Education from Converse College. Jennifer is currently a school librarian at the Edwin P. Todd School in Spartanburg, South Carolina. She has served as the president of the South Carolina Association of School Librarians and the Union County Carnegie Library Board of Trustees.

Index